Residential Roof Design

Using Autodesk® Revit®

Residential Roof Design

Using Autodesk® Revit®

For Beginning and Experienced Revit® Designers

Mark S. Sadler, RA, NCARB

 iUniverse®

**RESIDENTIAL ROOF DESIGN USING AUTODESK® REVIT®
FOR BEGINNING AND EXPERIENCED REVIT® DESIGNERS**

iUniverse books may be ordered through booksellers or by contacting:

iUniverse
1663 Liberty Drive
Bloomington, IN 47403
www.iuniverse.com
1-800-Authors (1-800-288-4677)

Because of the dynamic nature of the Internet, any web addresses or links contained in this book may have changed since publication and may no longer be valid. The views expressed in this work are solely those of the author and do not necessarily reflect the views of the publisher, and the publisher hereby disclaims any responsibility for them.

Any people depicted in stock imagery provided by Thinkstock are models, and such images are being used for illustrative purposes only. Certain stock imagery © Thinkstock.

ISBN: 978-1-5320-1686-8 (sc)
ISBN: 978-1-5320-1687-5 (e)

Library of Congress Control Number: 2017905375

Print information available on the last page.

iUniverse rev. date: 05/26/2017

To Kathy, who never stopped believing

Contents

Introduction

Have you ever started designing a home with Autodesk® Revit® and breezed through the walls, doors, and windows fairly quickly but then become frustrated at the difficulties you encountered when you got to the roof?

Maybe you've successfully used Revit to design commercial projects but you've put off tackling residential projects in Revit, believing they are too complex in their shapes, too loaded with custom detailing, to make them cost efficient in Revit.

Or perhaps you've heard that your competition is using Revit on their residential projects with favorable results and you wonder whether you're falling behind the curve.

If you are now or have been in any of these situations, I'm here to help. I want to assure you that these bumps in the road can be overcome. Revit can be a powerful and efficient tool for the design of houses, as well as other types of buildings that have house-like roofs.

A possible workflow for house design consists of these steps:

1. Use hand-drawn sketches to establish the general layout, room sizes, adjacencies, circulation, and feel of the house.
2. Create quick floor plans in Revit, using the hand sketches as underlays. At this stage, we can use generic 3-D elements (walls, doors, etc.) to true up dimensions and check square footages. As an alternate, CAD software can be used for this step.
3. From the 2-D plans, develop the Revit model in three dimensions, studying and tweaking the massing and spatial relationships. As we continue development of the design, we can add specific products, materials, and landscaping, allowing us to create quick 3-D presentations that get the clients excited and involved.
4. Produce accurate, internally consistent, and well-coordinated construction documents based on the 3-D model, using Revit's 2-D annotation tools.

Using Revit for presentations and client meetings can enhance the client experience far beyond any presentation involving only 2-D drawings. Designers are generally skilled at converting flat 2-D graphics into a 3-D mental picture, visible in their own imaginations. While clients may also have this ability, most of them have it to a lesser extent than the professionals who do it every day.

The people who come to designers for help are generally much more comfortable visualizing the world in three dimensions.

I firmly believe that the way of the future is toward increased collaboration and involvement by all the stakeholders in a building project. This includes architects, designers, engineers, contractors, community organizations, and owners. The forward-thinking designer will decide to lead this trend, not trail behind. One day the change-averse designer could find himself or herself struggling to catch up.

Revit is a natural fit for this trend of increased collaboration and communication. Better projects, increased productivity, and happier owners will be the result.

I hope this book encourages all residential architects, designers, and builders to embrace this still-new, still-developing technology to win more plum commissions and amaze their clients.

Using the techniques in this book, Revit-fluent designers will have the ability to produce realistic, quickly changeable, emotionally involving 3-D presentations that include the materials and detailing necessary to convey the style, beauty, and feel of the clients' future homes.

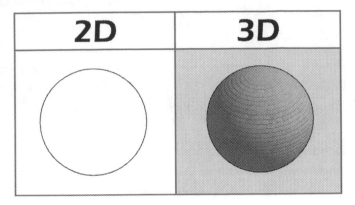

Figure 0.1. Which image would you say conveys more useful information?

Not Just for Making Pretty Pictures

The best part of this technology is that the visually impressive 3-D presentations flow naturally from the same virtual building model that yields the bulk of the two-dimensional views (plan, elevation, section, and schedules) that become the construction documentation. The model that is being developed during the design process becomes more and more enriched with information, which leads to consistent, accurate construction documents.

This flow of information is one of the key benefits to the Building Information Modeling (BIM) concept, of which Revit is the leading software product in today's market. In order to fully realize the benefits of BIM/Revit in residential projects, you will need to be able to model complex roofs with confidence.

This book will help you do that. It's designed for architects, designers, engineers, and builders who would like to create realistic, accurately modeled roofs for residential building projects. In reading this book and doing the exercises, it will be helpful if you already have a basic familiarity with Revit software, although even a total beginner will find this book to be a great primer for learning the basics.

Why am I confident that I have useful information and techniques to share? This book is based on many years of real-world and academic teaching experience. I've been a licensed architect for more than twenty-five years, practicing in various positions in many respected architectural, A/E, interior design, and design/build firms. I've designed and produced documents for a wide range of building types and learned a lot about construction methods, materials, and detailing. For more than seven years, I have taught college classes in Revit and AutoCAD.

When I'm not teaching college, I provide CAD/BIM/Revit training and consulting services for leading architectural, design, and construction companies, large and small. I help firms use Revit, AutoCAD, and other software efficiently to take their businesses to the next level.

I also produce a leading CAD blog called Best CAD Tips. I share lots of great information there relating to CAD and Revit. The address is www.bestcadtips.com.

I find great satisfaction in helping people grow in their mastery of the best tools, methods, and technology available, and by doing so, I help them reach their goals. In helping people gain confidence in useful and marketable skills, I know that I'm empowering them, in some small way, to find their best path in this rapidly changing world.

Figure 0.2. A fine residence modeled in Revit (Image courtesy of Plans By Design)

Giving you the tools you need to be more effective, creative, and productive is what this book is all about. I encourage you to learn all you can, practice unceasingly, and become the person who others turn to when the job must be done on time with the highest level of quality.

As you grow more confident with Revit, you'll find that it's one of the most enjoyable software tools out there. It's almost like building the house without ever hitting your thumb with a hammer. Here's to your success modeling houses and roofs in Revit!

Chapter 1

General Principles of Roof Modeling

The designer who uses Revit as his or her tool of choice faces a unique set of challenges when designing residential roofs. Part of this is due to the nature of the software, and part is just the nature of the roofs themselves.

Roofs are often the only elements of a building that are nonorthogonal or non–box shaped. Traditional-style houses generally make dramatic use of sloped roofs and overhangs to enhance the house's massing and silhouette. Roofs are a key part of any well-designed home's aesthetic. (The exception being the international style house, which hides its near-flat roofs from view behind parapet walls.) House roofs today tend to be complex in shape and highly detailed in a seemingly endless variety of ways.

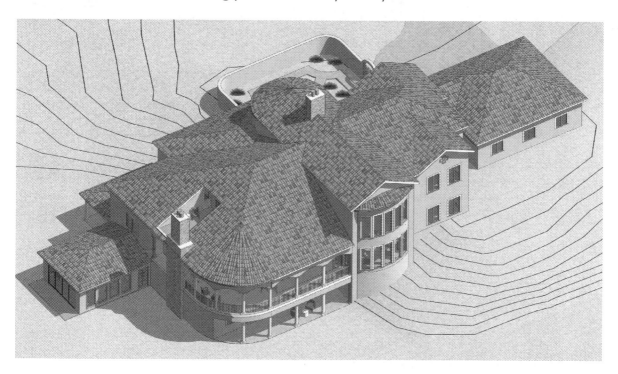

Figure 1.1. A complex roof in a Mediterranean-style residence
(Image courtesy of A.T.S. Design—Joseph Kirby)

This can be a challenge to a designer (or a design firm) looking to use Revit as their main software platform for residential design work.

At first glance, Revit seems to be better suited to designing commercial buildings than residential buildings. The orthogonal, boxy, ninety-degree-corner elements so common in commercial buildings go together with ease in Revit. On the other hand, traditional-styled houses, with their sloped, canted, curved, cranked, and custom-made elements, many inspired by centuries-old details, require more thought and attention. This is true in Revit, just as in the real world of construction.

It's important that the residential designer and his or her design team be well trained and apply some specific tools and techniques that address the challenges of residential projects. Primary among these are the procedures for modeling and detailing roofs contained in this book.

Roof Terminology

To make sure we are speaking the same language, let's begin by discussing some roof terminology.

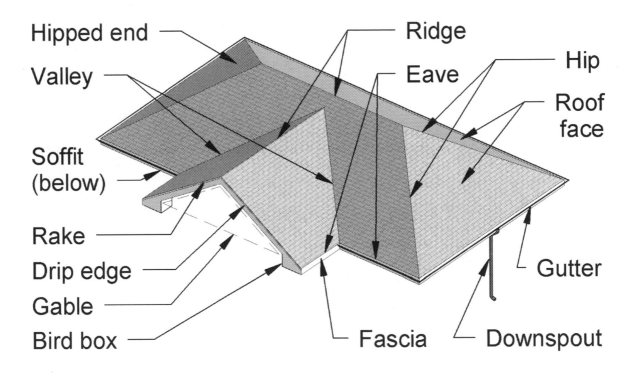

Figure 1.2. Roof terminology with illustration

Figure 1.2 shows the basic parts of a roof. A roof is made up of faces, edges, and trim.

Faces are generally planar and can be rectangular, triangular, or curved. Curved faces can be simple curves (like a barrel) or complex curves (like the shell of an egg).

Edges include ridges, hips, valleys, rakes, and eaves.

Trim includes gutters, downspouts, drip edges, flashing, fasciae, returns, crickets, saddles, and so on.

The term *gable* can refer to the overall roof shape, with two sloped faces meeting at a ridge, or to the triangular area formed within the end of a gable-shaped roof.

Hip is hard to define in words, easier to show in pictures. Often used to describe the overall roof shape, it actually refers to the sloping edge line where two roof faces that are not parallel to each other meet. *Merriam-Webster* defines hip in this way:

Hip: the external angle formed by the meeting of two sloping sides of a roof that have their wall plates running in different directions.

It's important to note that a *ridge* line runs true level, while a *hip* line runs at a slope. A *valley* is similar to a hip, except that its two faces meet in a concave shape rather than a convex shape.

Bird boxes are named for the benefit they provide of preventing birds from building nests in the front overhangs of a gable roof.

The *pitch* of a roof is the same as its *slope ratio*, for the purposes of this book.

An Excellent Invention, the Roof

Roofs were originally invented, I imagine, to keep rain from falling on the head of one of our very distant ancestors who was getting tired of living in a dark, dank cave.

If I had a time machine, I would like to go back and meet the inventor of the first-ever roof and shake his or her hand. Or, on second thought, maybe not.

Here's the unexpected thing about Revit roofs: rainwater falling on a real-world roof flows downhill, but Revit roofs grow uphill from their bottom edge or edges.

Rainwater on a real roof flows downhill, but roofs in Revit grow uphill.

When creating a roof in Revit, you start at the bottom (when you're using the Roof by Footprint tool) and let Revit work its way upward until reaching the ridge or peak.

The good news is that, as designers, we don't need to figure out exactly where the ridges, faces, valleys, or hip lines will end up. Revit will take care of that. We just draw a 2-D sketch of the roof's footprint and then designate which of the edge lines of the footprint are slope-defining edges. I like to think of these as slope-originating edges, since they are the originators of the upward slope of a roof face. We also need to tell Revit the *angle of slope* that we want for each of the slope-defining edges. This angle is usually expressed as a ratio of rise (height) to run (width). If we don't tell Revit our desired slope, it gives us a default slope of 9 inches of rise to 12 inches of run. Changing this slope is very easy.

It's helpful to think of Revit's slope-defining edges as the edges that rainwater flows toward. In other words, if you think of the slope-defining edges as the edges that would naturally have *gutters* installed along them, you're off to a good start.

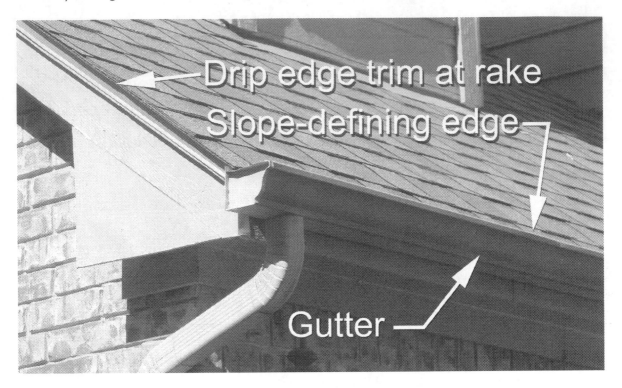

Figure 1.3. A raked edge and a slope-defining (guttered) edge

A raked edge of a gable roof, which runs parallel to the flow of rainwater, is not a slope-originating edge. Putting a gutter along a raked edge would be useless, since rainwater would generally not flow toward that edge. Rake edges typically receive a *drip edge*, which is a narrow, raised metal extrusion designed to protect the joint below from water damage. See figure 1.3.

A Roof's Best Friend: The Supporting Wall

Just as in the real world of construction, roofs in Revit depend upon the walls below them for alignment and positioning.

While it is possible to create roofs in Revit without justifying them to walls, using only sketched lines, I strongly recommend that you try to justify (constrain) your roofs to a supporting wall whenever you can.

Constraining roofs to walls, wherever such walls are available, makes the creation of roofs much easier, and—very importantly—it makes it easier to check your roof's geometry and determine if something needs adjustment. It also makes the slopes and overhangs easier to edit if needed. In short, it ensures that your roof is flexible and buildable.

Constraining roofs to supporting walls makes roof modeling much easier.

Getting to Know Sketch Mode

Sketch Mode is a crucial part of roof creation in Revit, and every Revit user should spend time getting to know it inside and out. Sketch Mode is a special environment where the designer creates the footprints and profiles that turn into three-dimensional objects when you click on the Big Green Checkmark. The 2-D lines of the sketch are magenta colored. All objects other than your sketch lines are grayed out and are not editable or selectable.

Sketch Mode Procedures

Each time you activate the Roof by Footprint tool, you are taken directly to Sketch Mode. You will see a Big Red X button and a Big Green Checkmark button below a green tab in the ribbon. See figure 1.4. All existing elements in the work area are shown in light gray. The new lines that you draw (your sketch) will be colored magenta.

Your task is to draw the roof's footprint, or outline, as a two-dimensional drawing.

The rules of drawing a roof footprint in Sketch Mode are as follows:

1. Lines must form closed loops—no gaps are allowed in a loop.
2. Lines must not cross or overshoot at corners, forming an X shape or a T shape.
3. Lines must not overlap or stack on top of other lines.
4. No stray lines are allowed that are not part of your loop.
5. More than two loops are not allowed.
6. Two loops are allowed but only if one loop is entirely inside of the other loop.
7. A loop inside of another loop creates a roof object with a hole in the middle of the roof. I think of this as a donut pattern, with a hole in the middle of a solid.

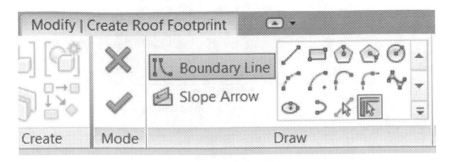

Figure 1.4. View of the ribbon in Sketch Mode

When you are done with your sketch, you exit Sketch Mode by clicking either the Big Green Checkmark or the Big Red X. See figure 1.4.

The Big Green Checkmark accepts your sketch, removes you from Sketch Mode, and converts the 2-D sketch into a 3-D roof object.

The Big Red X aborts the sketching operation, removes you from Sketch Mode, and your sketch is not saved.

After clicking on the Big Green Checkmark, the roof you created is automatically selected (displayed in blue) and ready for further editing if needed. To deselect the roof, simply click outside of the roof object in the work area, type [Esc] two times, or click on the Modify button in the ribbon.

Planning Your Work

Most large house designs require the creation of multiple Revit objects to model the roof. It's important to be able to analyze a roof design and mentally break it up into chunks or individual roof objects.

Generally, I like to model the larger chunks first. However, sometimes I start by modeling a smaller, simpler shape, such as a garage, because that can be done quickly, and it allows me to test my approach before moving on to the larger, more complex chunks of the project.

We will discuss chunking, or breaking a roof into separate parts, later.

Useful Views for Roof Design

Revit roof modeling requires constantly jumping between roof plan, elevation, section, and 3-D views. I usually close all windows except the two or three that I require for the roof object I'm currently modeling. Then I use Ctrl-Tab to cycle between the open windows.

You can also divide your work area into two or three tiled windows and move from one to another by clicking inside of the view you wish to activate. This way you can see your edits immediately in all views. The trade-off with this method is that the views are smaller.

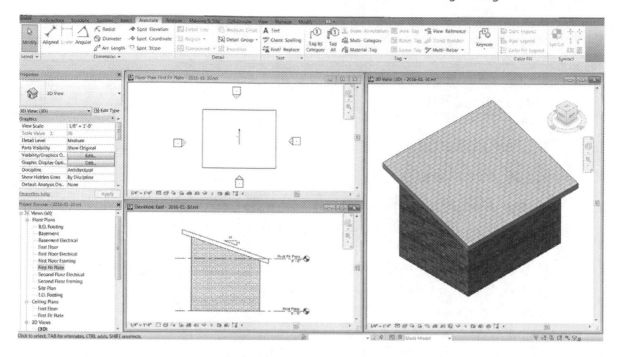

Figure 1.5. Split screen with three tiled views

To tile your views, simply open two or three desired views and go View tab > Windows panel > Tile. Your screen will look something like figure 1.5.

Saving and Copying Custom Roof Types

A *roof type* in Revit is an arrangement of one or more layers, which together form what I sometimes call a *roof assembly*. Think of it as a sandwich. This sandwich may include layers for shingles, metal panels, roofing felt, plywood sheathing, and a layer that represents a row of rafters—what I call the *rafter zone*. A generic roof type may have only one layer of nonspecified material; however, it must have a specified thickness.

Roofs in Revit are *system families*, which means they have certain rules and limitations that they share with other system families, including floors, walls, ceilings, and stairs.

Roof families and types cannot be saved as (RFA) family files in your office library. The best place to save a custom roof type that you want to use in future projects is in the template (RTE) file that you use to begin new projects.

What if the roof type that you need has been created but is saved in a different project? Copying a roof type from another project is easy. You use one of two methods:

1. Copy and paste a roof object using the Windows clipboard, or
2. Use Revit's Transfer Project Standards tool.

As with any system family, you can copy an *instance* of a roof type from Project A to Project B by using the Windows clipboard. Here's the procedure:

1. In Project A, go to the model and select the desired roof object by clicking on it.
2. Type Ctrl-C to copy the roof object to the Windows clipboard.
3. In Project B, go to a view similar to the one used in step 1, type Ctrl-V, and click at any desired location. The roof object will be placed at the location indicated. You will probably want to delete the roof object; it's served its purpose.
4. Now when you open the list of roof types, the imported roof type will appear in the list, ready to use in the current project.

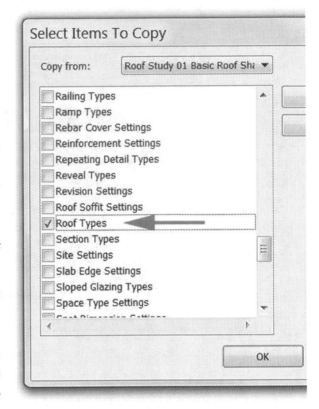

Figure 1.6. Transferring roof types from an outside project

The second method is to bring in the roof type (actually all the roof types) from Project A to Project B by using the Transfer Project Standards tool. Here is the procedure:

1. Open both Project A and Project B.
2. Go to Project B and go Manage tab > Settings panel > Transfer Project Standards button.
3. Verify that the Copy from: selector is set to copy from Project A.
4. In the Select Items to Copy dialog box, click on Check None.
5. Scroll down to find Roof Types in the list and check the box next to it. See figure 1.6.
6. Hit OK. All the roof types from Project A will now appear in the list of roof types in Project B.

The advantage of using the clipboard method over the Transfer Project Standards method is that with the first method you get only the roof type that you want. With the second method, you get all the types, whether you want them or not.

Is it the "Home" tab or the "Architecture" tab?

Throughout this book, I will refer to the far left ribbon tab containing the Build panel as the Architecture tab, since I am using Revit 2016. If you are using Revit Architecture, the same tab goes by the name "Home." Please substitute terms as needed.

We will do a lot of "hovering" in this book, so let's define the term. To "hover" means to place your pointer over something, without clicking, and watch for a visual change of some sort.

In the next chapter, we will learn how to set up level data for houses and save these in a custom Revit template.

Chapter 2

Setting Up a Custom Revit Template

One of the most important secrets to using Revit efficiently is to create and maintain a carefully crafted custom template and then use that template for beginning each new project. Making and maintaining your template takes time, but it pays huge dividends with future projects. A template for residential work will be very different from a commercial building template. Especially important is that you have wood-framed walls and roofs (with materials that are appropriate for your project's locality).

Elements of a great template include

- your most-used wall and roof types;
- most-used door and window types;
- level data ("data" in this context is the plural of datum, and a datum in Revit is either a level [visible in Elevation or Section view] or a grid line [visible in Plan view]);
- component families (such as cabinets and sinks) and model groups;
- 2-D detail components and detail groups; and
- wall, door, and window schedules set up the way you like them.

Generally it's best to create your custom template not by stripping down a recent project but by starting with a clean template file supplied by Autodesk and adding elements to it.

Try to keep your custom template lightweight and free of errors and warnings. Avoid having lots of images in your template, since they use lots of your computer's critical resources.

Maintaining your custom template file is a never-ending process. While no template is perfect, a good, up-to-date template will pay big dividends in time saved, compared to using a standard template.

Creating a Custom Revit Template

Start a new Revit project file. Go Big Blue R > New > Project.

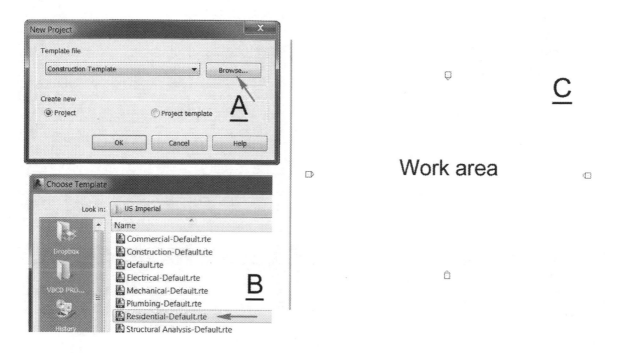

Figure 2.1. Starting a Residential Project

In the New Project box, for the Template file, click "Browse ..." as shown in figure 2.1-A.

At the Choose Template box, click on Residential-Default.rte, then hit Open. See figure 2.1-B.

Back in the New Project box, verify that the template file selector button says "Residential-Default.rte." Also verify that the radio button below the words "Create new" is set to "Project" (*not* Project template). Hit the OK button.

You should now have a work area with four elevation tags around an empty central area. See figure 2.1-C.

The Project Browser should show the First Floor view in bold font, indicating that it is the active view.

Next we need to customize the levels. Levels can only be seen and edited in Elevation or Section view. We don't have any section views yet, so let's open the South Elevation.

Open the South Elevation view in one of these ways:

- In the Project Browser, double-click the South Elevation's name under "Elevations Building Elevation."
- Hover over the triangular part of the elevation tag in the south part of the work area. When it turns blue, double-click on it.

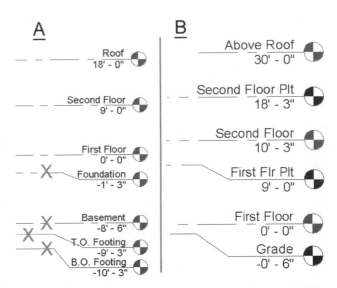

You will see default levels like those in figure 2.2-A. (These are shown compressed for better readability.)

Delete the five levels marked with Xs in figure 2.2-A. To do this, click on the level line (not the "target" symbol) to select the level, and then press the Delete key on the keyboard. You will get a warning as shown in figure 2.2-C. Click the OK button. You are deleting views along with the levels.

This is okay because we do not need those views. Plus, they are muddying up our views list. The various lists in Revit tend to grow long and complex, and it

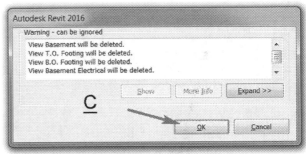

Figure 2.2. Customizing levels
for a two-story house

becomes mentally draining to repeatedly search through them. Anything we can do to eliminate useless (or seldom-used) items on our lists helps to preserve our mental energy, as well as boosting the Revit project file's compactness and speed.

Anything you can do to keep the various Revit lists short
and easy to search through is to your advantage.

For the next few steps, refer to figure 2.2-B.

1. Change the name of the Roof level to be "Above Roof," and change its height to 30'0". When Revit asks if you want to rename the corresponding views, click "No."
2. Create a new level called "First Flr Plate." To do this, select the First Floor level and use the Copy tool (CC is the hot key) to copy the level upward to a height of 9'0". Note that this new level's "target" symbol is black, unlike the blue color of the default levels. We'll discuss target symbol colors a bit later.
3. Copy the Second Floor level upward. Change the name of the new, copied level to be "Second Flr Plt" and set its height at 18'3". This represents the plate height for the second floor.

When you're done, the revised levels should look like figure 2.2-B (I've compressed the levels vertically for this illustration).

Setting the Roof Plan View Depth

Some adjustments are needed in the Roof Plan view in order to see what we want to see.

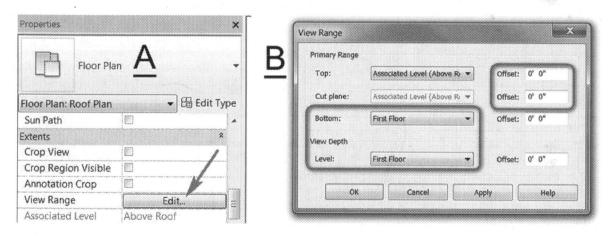

Figure 2.3. Setting the View Range for the Roof Plan view

Open the Roof Plan view. This is the plan view that is associated with the "Above Roof" level. In the Properties box, under Extents, click on View Range > Edit button. See figure 2.3-A.

In the View Range dialog, make the changes shown in figure 2.3-B. Change Top Offset to 0'0", change Cut Plane Offset to 0'0", change Bottom level to First Floor, and change View Depth level to First Floor. Click on Apply and OK to save your changes.

Something to remember: When I start to create a roof object while I am in the Roof Plan view, I must be sure to change the current work plane to match the *plate level* on which I want the roof to be supported. In construction terms, this is the plate on which the roof *bears*. If I forget to change the work plane, by default Revit will create the roof based on the Above Roof level, which means the roof will be floating 30 feet or so in the air. If I create a roof and it isn't visible in my roof plan, that is the first place that I look. I go to an Elevation or Default 3-D view, turn off the cropping, and type ZE (Zoom Extents). If you see a flying roof somewhere, it's probably mine.

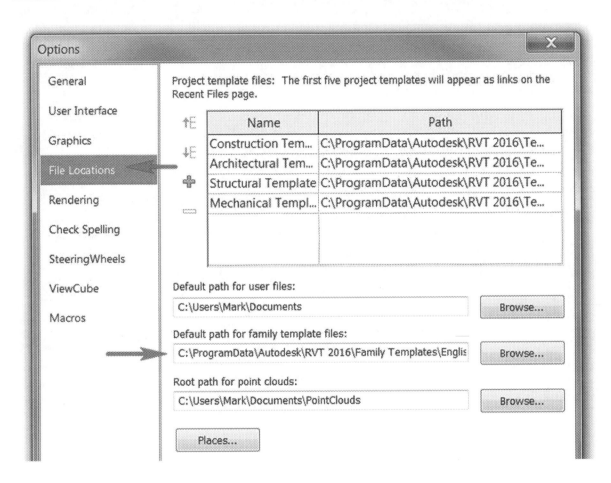

Figure 2.4. The File Locations tab in the Options box

This would be a good time to save the revised levels in a template (RTE) file for use in future projects. Just click on Big Blue R > Save As > Template. Give the template a descriptive name, such as "My Excellent Residential Template," and click on Save. Save the RTE template file to an easy-to-find location.

If you want, you can add your custom template to the template file folder that Revit goes to by default when you start a new project. Be aware, however, if you save it there; your custom template may not appear in the same location the next time you upgrade Revit to a new version. Keep a backup copy of the file handy in your own personal library folder.

To save your template to the default Revit template folder, click the Big Blue R > Options button > File Locations tab. A dialog box opens similar to figure 2.4.

Under Project Template Files, click on the Path for Architectural Template. This will tell you the path to the project template files folder if you delete the "default.rte" at the end of the path.

After you save your template file, be sure to close the template file. You don't want to begin working on a new project while you are still in your RTE template file; that can lead to thorny issues.

Black and Blue "Target" Symbols

It's best to create a level datum for every plate height in the project.

In some projects, this can lead to a lot of levels. That's okay. I still recommend it, because when you model a roof, it's much easier and less confusing if you have a level datum dedicated to the top of the wall on which that roof will bear. It just makes your life easier.

Create a level datum for every plate height in the project.

When creating a level for a plate, I always use the Copy command to create the level datum, rather than clicking on the Level button in the Datum panel of the ribbon. Why? By default, the Level tool automatically creates multiple associated plan views (floor plan, ceiling plan, and structural plan), which (for a plate) are unnecessary and confusing. I don't want my list of views to be muddied up with unneeded views. If you accidentally begin using the Datum > Level tool in the ribbon but realize you don't want to create any new views, you can look in the Options bar and uncheck the Make Plan View option (see figure 2.5-B).

You can discern by the colors of the target symbols which levels were created by the Level button in the ribbon; they have a blue target symbol. The levels with black target symbols were created by copying an existing level.

Figure 2.5-A shows another set of levels from a two-story house project. Note that only the levels tied to *actual building floors* have blue-colored targets. (This house has an elevated game room, which called for an extra level at 2'0" above the second floor.) All the non-building-floor-level target symbols are black, meaning that no "junk" plan views were created when making the level data by using the Copy tool.

In the Project Browser, keep the list of views clean and concise.

The Horizontal Section Tool

Sometimes in modeling a house, I need a more flexible, all-purpose plan detail view. I may want to see the plan view I would get if I cut a section horizontally through the building at some height other than four feet above a floor level.

That is why, in addition to the levels shown above, I often create a special, moveable level called Horizontal Section. See figure 2.6-C.

This level is intended to be moved as needed to any height that I choose, cutting a plan view through the part of the building I'm working on at the time. This is especially helpful for dormers and cupolas.

For example, if I'm modeling a roof cupola, I'll go to an elevation view and move the Horiz Section level up or down as needed to cut through the window openings of the cupola. See figure 2.6-B. Similarly, when designing a dormer, the plan view might look like figure 2.6-A. If you later decide to make the cupola or dormer plan view permanent, you will need to set up a permanent level for it at the appropriate height.

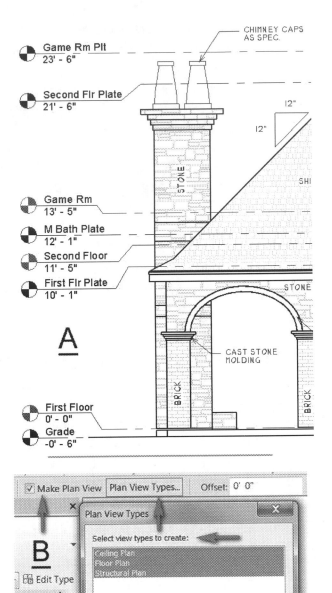

Figure 2.5. Levels for a two-story residence

16

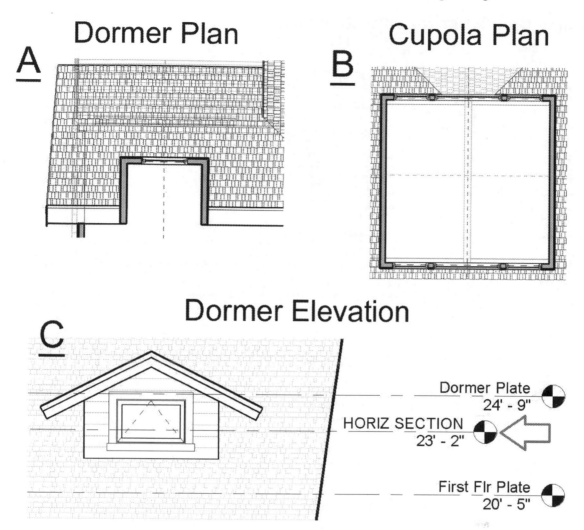

Figure 2.6. Using a Horizontal Section level to study a dormer or cupola in plan

Here is the procedure for making a variable-height Horizontal Section view:

1. Create a new level called Horiz Section by copying an existing level to any height desired.
2. Click on View tab > Create panel > Plan Views pull-down menu > Floor Plan button. You will be taken to the New Floor Plan dialog box as shown in figure 2.7-A.
3. Select Horiz Section level from the list. Hit OK. You should now be in the newly created Horiz Section view.
4. With nothing selected, go to Properties box and adjust the View Range as described below.

Setting Up the Horizontal Section View

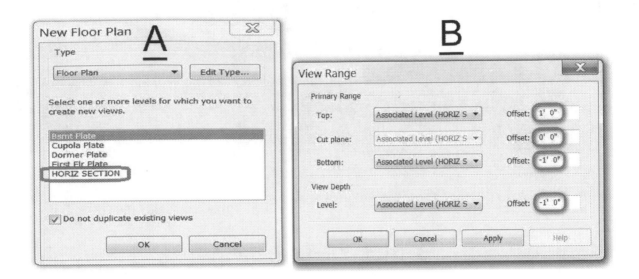

Figure 2.7. The view range of a Horizontal Section

In the View Range settings, the plan view associated with this level should have a *zero offset* for the cut plane, so that when I place the level line at my desired height in an elevation view, the plan view cuts through the walls and windows at *exactly* the height at which the level line is set. You do not want the typical four-foot offset from the floor level. See figure 2.7-B.

There is one potential issue to watch out for when you're using this Horizontal Section Level tool. If you're not careful, objects tend to attach themselves to it when you don't want them to.

Revit typically associates an object's height (such as a wall or a window) with the currently active view's work plane. That means when you are using the Horiz Section view, objects you create may become attached to it. You may notice a window or wall (for example) moving out of its correct position when you move the Horiz Section level to a different height. Here are ways to prevent this from happening:

- Keep the Horiz Section level datum far up above the roof's peak when it's not being used.
- Take special care in setting the *current work plane* when creating or placing new elements (such as windows or walls) while in this Horiz Section plan view. Check and recheck the current work plane setting by going to Architecture tab > Work Plane panel > Set and set the work plane to an appropriate, nonchanging level.
- When you are done working on your dormers, move the Horiz Section level to a location slightly above the roof and see whether any objects remain attached to it and rise along with it. If so, select the objects and attach them to a permanent level instead.

In the next chapter, we will model a small building and study the roof-to-wall connections.

Chapter 3

Modeling a Pump House

We will now create a small, simple building to study Revit's capabilities. Let's start by modeling a small rectangular building—a pump house.

First, start a new project (Big Blue R > New > Project). In the New Project dialog box, when Revit gives you the opportunity to select a template file (see figure 2.1-A), browse to the custom template file that you created in chapter 2 (this is important). Click OK to start the new project.

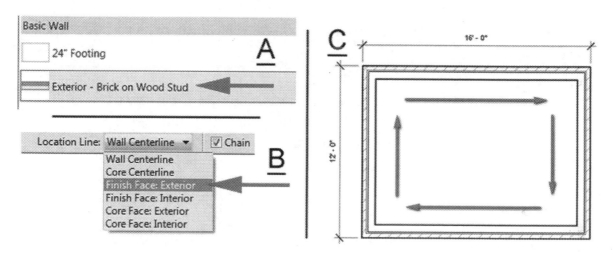

Figure 3.1. Modeling the building walls

Now we're ready to model our pump house. In Floor Plan view:

1. Click on Architecture tab > Build panel > Wall button. (It's not necessary to pull down the flyout menu under the Wall button, but if you do, choose Wall – Architectural.)
2. In the Properties box, in the selector pane, pull down the options for the Wall Type, and under the Basic Wall category, select Exterior – Brick on Wood Stud. See figure 3.1-A.
3. In the Properties box, set the Top Constraint to be Up to level: First Floor Plate. Click on the Apply button.
4. In the Options bar, set the Location Line at Finish Face: Exterior. See figure 3.1-B.
5. In the work area, in the space between the four elevation markers, draw a rectangular building sixteen feet by twelve feet as shown in figure 3.1-C, moving in a clockwise direction.

Thanks to Revit's highly intuitive drawing tools, you don't need to be concerned about turning Ortho on, typing in the lengths of the walls, commanding an endpoint snap, or trimming the corners. Just watch the blue temporary dimensions, use the default "magnetic" alignment and snap tools, and stay close to the dotted blue alignment lines.

To see all the layers in the walls, go to the Status Bar below the bottom left corner of the work area and change the Detail Level to Fine.

The walls are done! Now we're ready to create a roof.

Creating the Roof Footprint

In the Project Browser, go to the Roof Plan view under Floor Plans. You are looking down on the walls from above. If you don't see your building walls, go back to figure 2.3-B to see how to correct the View Depth settings.

To start the roof-making tool, go to Architecture tab > Build panel > Roof button and click it. You do not need to open the flyout menu, since Revit chooses Roof by Footprint by default. However, if you do open the flyout menu, you want to choose Roof by Footprint.

Since the setting for Slope Defining is *on* by default, it saves
time if we create the slope-defining edges first and then
turn that option *off* to create the other edges.

There are several settings that you need to change or verify before sketching the roof:

1. In the green-colored Modify | Create Roof Footprint tab, make sure that the Pick Walls tool is selected as shown in figure 3.2-A.
2. In the Options bar, verify that "Defines slope" is checked, as shown in figure 3.2-B.
3. In the Options bar, change the Overhang dimension setting to 1'6".
4. In the Options bar, check the option for "Extend to wall core."
5. In the Properties box, in the Selector Pane, pull down the roof types and select Basic Roof/ Wood Rafter 8" – Asphalt Shingle.
6. In the Properties box, under Constraints, verify that Base Level is set to First Floor Plate.

Whew! That may seem like a lot of settings, but what we've actually done is the following:

1. Initiated the Pick Walls tool, constraining the roof's edges to the selected walls. This is necessary for the Overhang function to work.
2. Turned on the Slope Defining option for the next edge line drawn.
3. Set the desired overhang dimension, a critical part of the roof's aesthetics.
4. Told Revit to measure the overhang dimension from the outside face of the wall's stud zone (if "Extend to wall core" is *on*), or from the exterior finish face of the wall (if turned *off*).
5. Selected the desired roof type—shingles, metal roof, rafter depth, and so on.
6. Verified the correct level to attach the roof to—a common source of problems when working in Roof Plan view.

You might ask, how can the roof be attached (or constrained) to both the wall and to the level datum? Simply put, if the wall moves horizontally, the roof's edge will move horizontally with it, and if the level datum moves vertically, the roof will move vertically with the level datum.

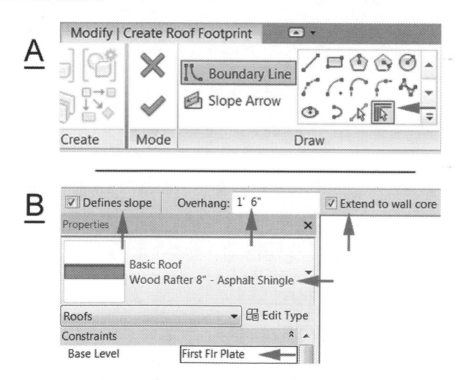

Figure 3.2. Preparing to create a roof using the Pick Walls tool

Now you're ready to actually draw the 2-D footprint of the roof in Sketch Mode.

Creating a One-Direction Sloped Roof

1. Hover over the north wall, making sure that the light-blue dotted preview line is *outside of* the building, not inside. See figure 3.3-A.
2. Click on the north wall. You'll now see a magenta line outside of the building wall. There should be a triangle and a slope ratio visible near the edge line. See figure 3.3-B.
3. This default slope (9" / 12") is most likely not the slope that you want. With the edge line still selected, click on the blue text object near the magenta triangle. You should now be in Text Editing mode (white letters on blue background). All the text should be selected automatically.
4. Type 4 [ENTER]. This is the fastest way to change the slope from 9" / 12" to 4" / 12".

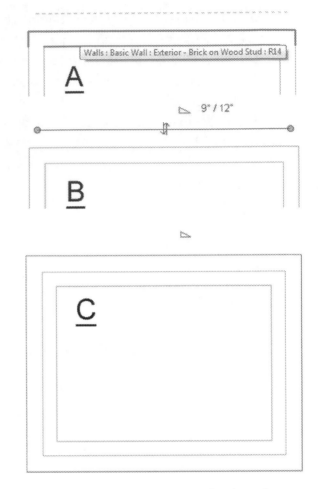

Figure 3.3. Creating a shed roof

Speed tip: typing the desired inch number and then [ENTER] is the fastest way of changing the slope of an edge or of a roof.

---

5. In the Options bar, *uncheck* the "Defines Slope" option. This affects the edge lines you're about to create.
6. Click on the other three walls, moving in a clockwise direction. These lines should *not* have a triangle next to them. You should now have a closed loop of magenta-colored lines similar to figure 3.3-C.
7. Click on the Big Green Checkmark to accept the sketch and create the 3-D roof. The roof is selected (and displayed in blue) automatically.
8. Click anywhere outside of the roof object to deselect it. Your roof is created.

Speed tip: all you need to do to change the slope, once
you are in text editor mode, is type 4 [ENTER].

Viewing the Roof in 3-D

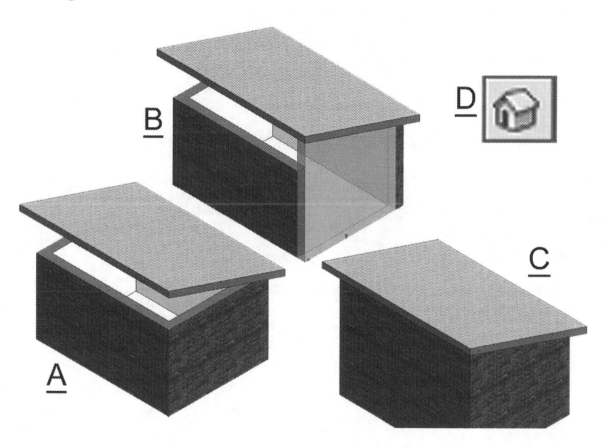

Figure 3.4. Attaching a wall to a roof

In the Project Browser, double-click on the default 3-D view, named {3-D}. As an alternate, you can click on what I call the "Doghouse" button (figure 3.4-D) in the Quick Access Toolbar at the top of the screen. This also opens the Default 3-D view.

After changing the Visual Style to *Realistic*, your building should look like figure 3.4-A.

To keep the birds from flying in, let's attach the walls to the roof. Click the right wall to select it.

In the ribbon, go Modify | Walls > Modify Wall > Attach Top/Base. Click on the roof (be sure to click on the linework at the roof's edges) and you should see something like figure 3.4-B.

Click in empty space to deselect the wall, or click the Modify button at the left end of the ribbon. Repeat the procedure to attach the other three walls, as shown in figure 3.4-C. No birds!

Orbiting around Your Building

Now that we have modeled the roof, I always like to orbit around the model, almost as if it were a physical model that you can turn in your hands.

Holding down [SHIFT] while pressing down on the *mouse wheel* and moving the mouse on your desktop lets you orbit the model.

Save time by setting up a five-button mouse for 3-D orbiting.

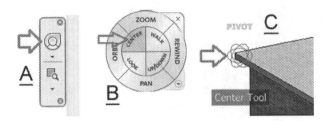

Figure 3.5. Setting the pivot point for orbiting

I save lots of time by using a five-button mouse and programming one of the side buttons to be equivalent to the "middle button," which is the same as holding down the mouse wheel. Then I hold down the Shift key while pressing the side mouse button to orbit around the model. It's much easier than pressing down the mouse wheel.

You can also use the Steering Wheel to orbit. The Steering Wheel is in the navigation bar at the upper-right side of your work area (see figure 3.5-A). Click on the Steering Wheel icon, and the Steering Wheel tool will follow your pointer around on the screen, like an adoring puppy.

To set the center point, or pivot point, of the orbiting tool, *hover* over the Center button of the steering wheel, as shown in figure 3.5-B. Then click and drag, holding down the mouse button, until the green ball-shaped Pivot icon is over a point in the model that Revit can easily snap to, such as a corner point of your roof. Release your mouse button to place the pivot point. See figure 3.5-C. The view will pan to place your orbit point in the exact center of your work area.

Now whenever you use the Orbit tool, that pivot point will stay anchored to its spot in the center of your screen.

This is great, because it prevents the model from flying off into outer space when you try to orbit around it. It makes it easy to zoom in and inspect a small area that you want to study.

In the next chapter, we will learn how to make a well-designed supporting wall for your roof to bear on.

Chapter 4

Customizing Roof and Wall Assemblies

It's always best to start with well-designed walls for our Revit roofs to connect to and spring upward from.

In the residential construction world, the height of the exterior wall's top plate above the floor is a critical dimension that controls the height of the ceilings, upper floors, and roofs. This *plate height* dimension is a critical part of the construction documents for any house.

In Revit, the plate height is just as crucial. Revit makes it easy to use a level datum to mark this critical dimension, and then use it to model the roof-to-wall connection. A great deal of this work is done in Section view.

A great roof needs a great wall to spring from.

I think of the Section view as the tattletale view in Revit! You may have a great-looking model as viewed from the building's exterior, but if you go to Section view and find that the roof-to-wall connection is fouled up, your roof could be entirely in the wrong place. This calls into question the accuracy of the whole model.

If the wall locations are true, the plate heights are true, and the roof-to-wall connections are good, you can be confident that the roofs at least have a good starting point.

Ask any builder—the best way to ensure that you get a strong, stable roof is to start with a strong, stable wall and make a good roof-to-wall connection. The same is true in Revit!

To demonstrate how to make a successful roof-to-wall connection, we will continue working on the pump house building that we created in chapter 2.

If the exterior wall's plate heights are correct, and the roof-to-wall connections are correct, you can bet that the roofs are also correct.

Let's cut a section through the building. In the First Floor Plan, place a section tag as shown in figure 4.1-A.

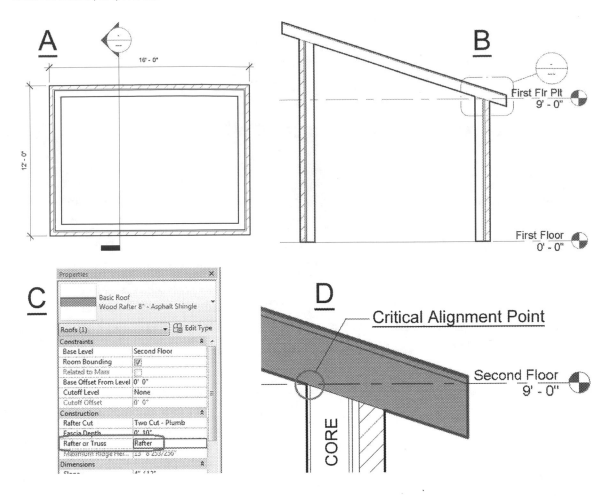

Figure 4.1. Plan and section views of roof-wall connection

The resulting Section view looks like figure 4.1-B.

Now we will create a Detail Section view. Go View tab > Create panel > Callout flyout menu > Rectangle. Draw the callout boundary as shown in figure 4.1-B.

To open the new view, you can either

1. look under Sections in the project browser for the view named Section 1 – Callout 1 or
2. just double-click on the bubble of the callout tag.

Change the Scale setting in the callout view to 1" = 1'0", and set the Detail level to Fine.

In this exercise, we are going to assume we are building the roof with rafters, not trusses. We notice that the rafters are sitting too high above the wall in this detail section. This happened because the Rafter or Truss setting in Properties defaults to Truss, which is not what we want. We will now change the setting to Rafter.

1. In the detail section view, select the roof.
2. In Properties, under Construction, change the Rafter or Truss setting to Rafter. See figure 4.1-C. Hit Apply.

3. The roof drops down slightly, and now the rafter-to-stud wall alignment looks better. See the Critical Alignment Point in figure 4.1-D.
4. Click in empty space in the work area to deselect all objects—or hit the Modify button at the left end of the ribbon.

We will discuss the Critical Alignment Point in more detail later in this chapter. We now have the roof aligning properly with the stud wall that supports it. However, the wall itself could stand some improvement.

Making a New, Optimized Wall Type

In order to improve the detail view of the connection between the roof and the wall, we need a more optimized wall type. I generally prefer that my exterior wall types have a total thickness measured in even inches with no fractions, like 10" or 12". It makes designing a building a lot simpler.

Fractions are not your friends. Any time you can eliminate them, you are helping the design team as well as the builder.

The air space behind the brick layer, or the stucco layer in a stucco wall, is usually a good place to make a thickness adjustment in order to eliminate fractions in the overall assembly.

Let's make a new, optimized wall type. Revit allows the creation of wall types by a simple method:

1. Select an existing wall type that closely resembles the wall you want.
2. Duplicate the wall type.
3. Rename the new wall type with a brief descriptive name.
4. Modify the physical characteristics of the new wall type as desired.

Here's the step-by-step procedure:

Start the Wall tool, or just select one of the existing walls. Be sure the wall type is displayed in the Selection Pane of the Properties dialog box. You want to select the existing wall type that is *most similar* to the wall type you want. I will just select one of the walls of my model.

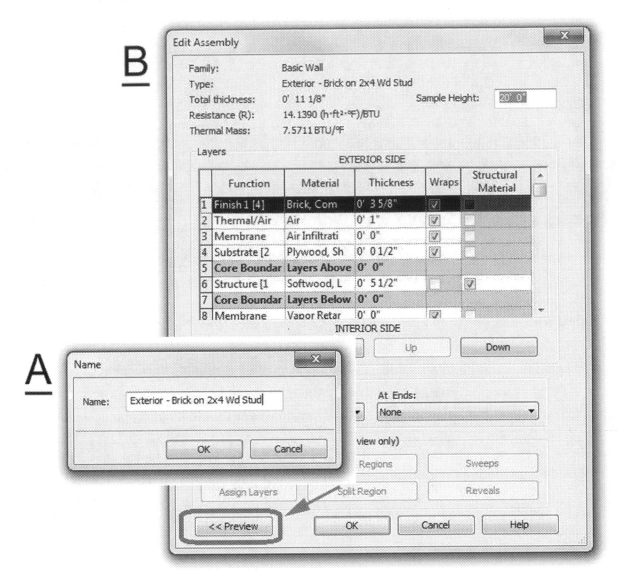

Figure 4.2. New wall settings

In the Properties box, below the selector pane, click on Edit Type.

In the Type Properties box, click Duplicate ...

In the Name box, give the new wall type a unique name that is brief yet descriptive. I will call the new wall type "Exterior – Brick on 2x4 Wd Stud." I always delete the annoying "[Space] 2" at the end of every new name. See figure 4.2-A. Hit OK.

Back in the Type Properties box, click the button next to Structure called Edit ...

You are now in the Edit Assembly dialog box.

This dialog box contains an *abundance* of useful tools, information, and settings. It deserves careful study. We will only go over a few essential points here.

Open the Preview window by clicking the <<Preview button in the bottom left corner. See figure 4.2-B.

Stretch the borders of the dialog box horizontally to make it more legible. Hover over the right border of the dialog box and watch for the double arrow symbol. Click and drag the double arrow to the right.

Stretch the column widths as needed to make them legible. Hover over the vertical black line between the column headings (such as Material and Thickness) and watch for the double arrow. Click and drag the double arrow to adjust the column widths.

Adjusting the Wall's Layers

Now we're ready to change the physical characteristics of the wall.

I want to create a 2x4 stud wall with brick veneer, with at least 1 1/2 inches of air space between the sheathing and the brick. I also want the wall's overall thickness to be even inches, no fractions allowed. This will make my floor plan dimensioning work out much better.

Here is the procedure to make the improved wall type. Refer to figure 4.3.

1. Starting at the top of the table, which is the Exterior Side, Row 1 is the brick layer. It is perfect, except for the unlovable color of the brick. We will let that remain as it is for now.
2. Row 2 is the air layer. I'll change this to 1 1/2 inches, my desired minimum.
3. Rows 3, 4, and 5 are fine—no change.
4. Row 6 needs to be changed to 3 1/2 inches for a 2x4 stud wall.
5. Rows 7, 8, and 9 are fine—no change.

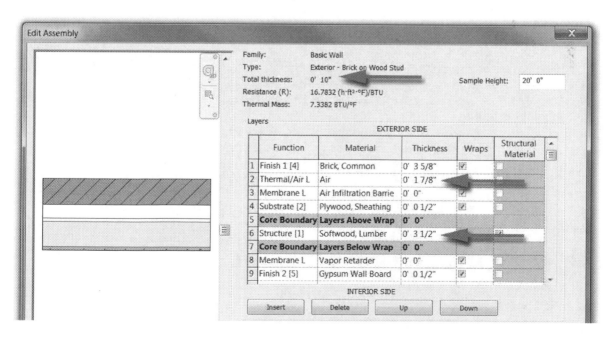

Figure 4.3. Editing the wall assembly

Looking at the top of the dialog box, I see that the Total thickness is 0'9 5/8". Since I want an even-inch overall wall thickness, I need to add 3/8" to one of the layers. The most flexible layer to change is the Air layer (the cavity behind the brick layer). Returning to layer 2, I change the thickness of the Air layer from 1 1/2" to 1 7/8". The Total thickness of the wall now reads 10"—perfect.

Click OK on this box. Then click OK on the Type Properties box. Done! The wall that you selected in your model should now show the new wall type name in the Properties dialog box.

Use the Match Properties tool (the hot key for this very useful tool is MA) to paint the new wall type onto the other building walls.

Figure 4.4 shows eight of my favorite wall types for residential design. These are set up to eliminate fractions in the overall thickness of the walls. They can easily be converted into simplified two-layer exterior wall types (discussed later in this chapter).

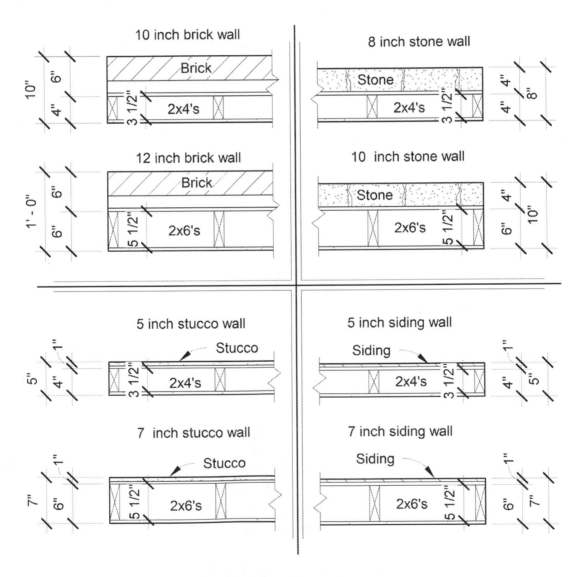

Figure 4.4. Some of my favorite exterior wall types

Editing the Roof Assembly

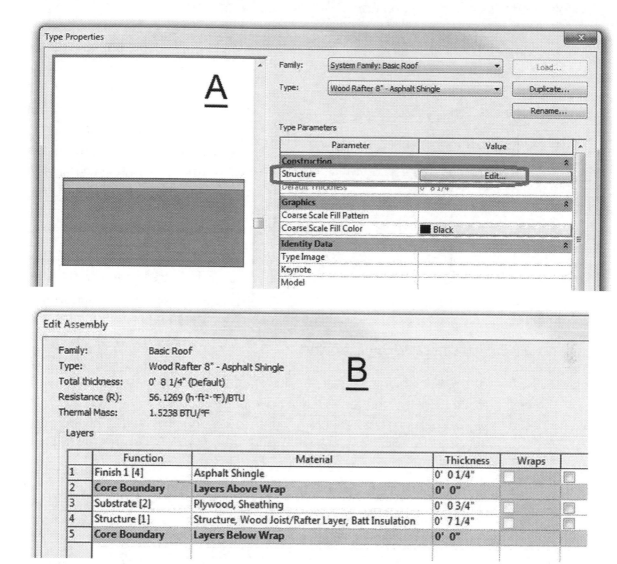

Figure 4.5. New roof settings

Now let's look closely at the structure of the roof assembly itself. In Revit, the word *structure* in the Type Properties table has a meaning that's very different from the same word in the construction world. *Structure* in the Type Properties dialog box means the order, thicknesses, and material properties of the layers that make up the roof type.

When you select a roof object in your model, the basic settings for that *instance* of the roof are shown in the Properties box. Click on the Edit Type … button, and it takes you to the Type Properties dialog box, as shown in figure 4.4-A.

Click Structure – Edit … and you are taken to the Edit Assembly dialog box. See figure 4.4-B.

The top rows of the table are, naturally, the upper layers of the roof assembly, or what I call the roof "sandwich." The bottom rows are at the lower layers of the assembly. The structurally strong layers of this roof type are rows 3 and 4, the Plywood Sheathing and Wood Joist/Rafter layers. These two Core layers are bracketed, top and bottom, by the two gray-colored Core Boundary rows.

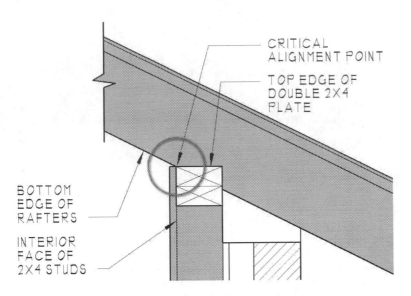

The Core Boundary rows are nonphysical layers. They are always zero thickness. Their position in the roof assembly allows the designer to tell Revit (and other Revit users) which layer(s) the designer considers to be the structural Core of the roof assembly.

In creating a roof, we want to make sure that the roof structure (the core) is bearing properly on the top plate of the wall.

Figure 4.6. Critical alignment point

In the real world of construction, the bottom edge of each rafter gets notched so that it meets the top-interior edge of the wall plate perfectly at the top-interior edge of the notch. I call this the "Critical Alignment Point." I've circled this point in figure 4.6. It is from this point that the roof springs upward. The part of the roof sloping downward from this point can be controlled in Revit by the Overhang settings.

The Critical Alignment Point is the point in Section view where the roof rafters spring upward from the *interior edge* of the wall's top plate.

Note that Revit does not model individual rafter boards in its roofs—only a rafter zone. Similarly, the walls in Revit do not contain individual studs—just a stud zone that can be set to the width of the studs—usually 3 1/2" or 5 1/2".

The rafter zone can be set to any thickness, depending on the size of rafters chosen by the designer or engineer. I think it's a good idea to make the rafter zone thickness realistic while limiting the number of different rafter thicknesses to a small number within a given project.

You can find a list of standard wood framing members in Revit. Just go to the 2-D drawing tools. Click on Annotate tab > Detail panel > Component flyout > Detail Component > Dimension Lumber – Section.

Typical wood framing sizes are:

Nominal	Thickness	Width
2x2	1 1/2"	1 1/2"
2x4	1 1/2"	3 1/2"
2x6	1 1/2"	5 1/2"
2x8	1 1/2"	7 1/4"
2x10	1 1/2"	9 1/4"
2x12	1 1/2"	11 1/4"

Rafter sizes typically range from 2x6 to 2x12.

Since the thickness of the rafter zone affects the ridge height and the way that roofs intersect walls and other elements, it's good to set the rafter zone thickness early in the modeling process. Better yet, create a few office-standard, typical roof types and save them in a custom Revit template file for use in new residential projects.

Matching real-world rafter depths in your model can be time-consuming.

It may be most time-efficient to assume one standard rafter zone thickness (say, for example, 5 1/2") and stick with it for all roofs, no matter what. The benefits to be gained by accurately modeling all the various rafter depths in a project may not be worth the time required. If a structural engineer is involved in the project, he or she would probably want to accurately model each rafter zone thickness, and the structural Revit model can be linked into the architectural model.

If the exact ridge height is needed to ensure compliance with local ordinances, you will need to model the roof assembly with a higher degree of accuracy.

You will need to create a separate roof type for each thickness of the rafter zone.

Keep the Rafter Undersides Unfinished

I have found that it is not helpful to include a bottom finish layer, such as a plywood soffit or a gypsum board ceiling, as part of the roof assembly. If you do this, Revit ignores the Core Boundary layers and makes the bottom edge of the soffit layer bear on the top-interior corner of the plate. It's not difficult to manually move the roof object downward, but it would be better if Revit respected the Core Boundary settings when placing the roof.

Another thing to consider: if you include a ceiling layer (such as gypsum board) attached to the rafters in a roof assembly, Revit considers the ceiling finish layer as part of the roof, not as a ceiling. As a result, ceiling-hosted light fixtures will not attach to or recess into it. In general, I've found it's better to add the ceiling layer as a separate object, in the Ceiling category. This applies to second-floor assemblies as well. I hope that Autodesk will work on this and allow a Ceiling-category bottom layer to be part of a Roof or Floor assembly.

Including ceiling or soffit finish layers as part of the roof assembly can lead to issues.

Making a New Roof Assembly Type

We will now create a new roof type with a 5 1/2" rafter zone depth. Since roofs types are system families, we must start with an existing roof type and then duplicate, rename, and edit the type.

Here are the steps:

1. Open the Revit file created in the exercise in the previous chapter.
2. Select the roof. The Properties box shows that it is a Wood Rafter 8" – Asphalt Shingle roof type.
3. Click on Edit Type, then Duplicate ...
4. For the name, change it to "Wood Rafter 6" – Asphalt Shingle."
5. Click on Structure – Edit ... to open the Edit Assembly dialog box. See figure 4.7-A.
6. Change the Plywood Sheathing thickness to 1/2".
7. Change the Wood Joist/Rafter thickness to 5 1/2".
8. Hit OK, then OK at the Type Properties dialog box. Done.

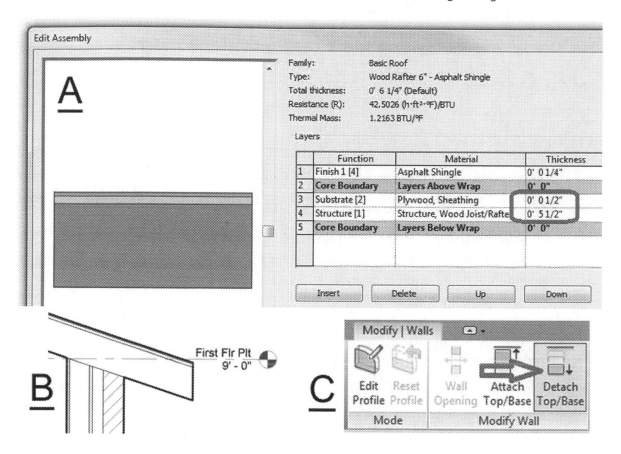

Figure 4.7. Tweaking the roof assembly and wall connection

Returning to the Section 1 – Callout 1 view, we now have something like figure 4.7-B. But wait—there's something funny about this section. The top of the wall assembly should not be cut off at the angle of the roof slope! That doesn't happen in the real world. We need to detach the wall from the roof to make this section look more realistic.

Detaching Walls from the Roof

The next step in adding realism and detail to the project is to detach the wall from the roof. Yes, earlier we used the Attach Top/Base tool to attach the walls to the roof. That was a good way to quickly get the exterior views to look good. However, when it's time to create a more realistic detail section view, we need to detach the roof and then fine-tune the roof-to-wall connection.

Here's the procedure for detaching a wall from a roof:

1. Select the wall in the Callout 1 view. (The scale of the view is 1" = 1'0".)
2. Click on the Detach Top/Base button in the green part of the ribbon. See figure 4.6-C.
3. Next, click on the roof that the wall is attached to. Be sure to click the linework, not the open area in the middle.
4. The wall is now detached from the roof.

However, we have work to do. See figure 4.8-B. We can see that the brick layer is intruding into the rafter zone—not ideal. We also note that there is only one shape handle (the blue triangle) at the top of the wall. That means we need to create one or more *extendible wall layers*.

Making Wall Layers Extendible

Revit allows the wall's layers to be split into a main part and an extendible part. Each part gets its own shape handle and can be controlled independently. The advantage of this is that

- your section views look more realistic and
- the brick layer can be lowered so that it does not poke through the house's roof and make an unsightly distraction in 3-D views.

We can choose one or more contiguous (touching) wall layers and give them a *height offset* from the main part of the wall. The offset dimension can be positive (upward) or negative (downward). In this case, we want to pull the top of the brick layer downward.

This extending can be set separately at both the top and bottom of the same wall. The layers do not have to match at the top and bottom. At the bottom, the extension can allow the brick to go down to the bottom of a brick ledge. Here, we're mainly interested in how the wall joins the roof.

Here is the procedure to modify the wall layers so that the top of the brick layer can be offset from the top of the stud wall:

1. Select an instance (any instance) of the wall type you want to modify. This can be in any view.
2. Go Properties > Edit Type > Structure – Edit ...
3. Open the Preview window and switch the setting to Section: Modify type.
4. Click the Modify button. See figure 4.8-A.
5. Click once inside the Preview window to activate the window. Now pan and zoom to get to the top of the wall, with a close-in zoomed view.
6. Select the *top edge* of the brick layer by clicking on it in the Preview window. A blue lock symbol will appear. See figure 4.8-A.
7. *Unlock* the layer's top edge by clicking on the lock symbol. It should now appear unlocked (open).
8. Repeat the unlocking process for the Air layer and the Plywood Sheathing layer. You can use the "hover-Tab-click" method to select the smaller lines.
9. Be sure that the unlocked layers are contiguous (touching each other). Revit does not allow noncontiguous layers to be unlocked. Membrane layers do not count in this procedure, since they have zero thickness.
10. Hit OK, then Apply and OK until you get back to the work area.

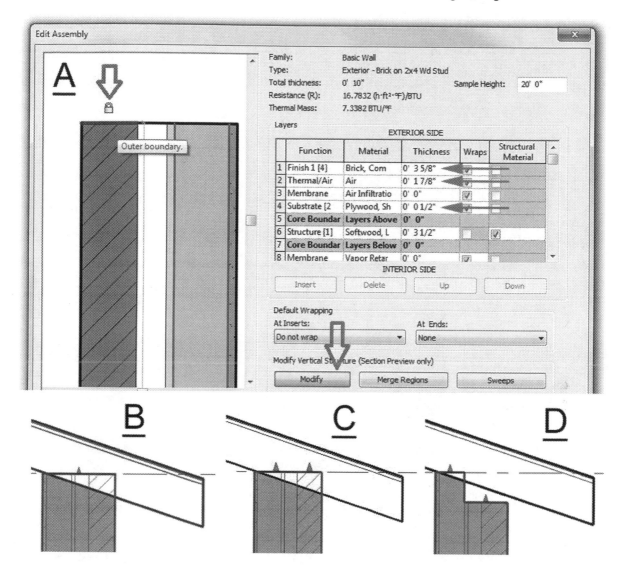

Figure 4.8. Making wall layers extendible

Now your wall should have *two* shape handles, because we made the outer layers extendible. See figure 4.8-C.

Click and drag on the right (brick) layer's shape handle and pull it downward to below the bottom of the rafter.

See figure 4.8-D. This looks *much* better!

Mark S. Sadler, RA, NCARB

Making a Simplified Two-Layer Wall

Some designers may feel that the wall type we created above is more complex than they need. After all, many hand-drawn or CAD-drawn residential floor plans show only two layers in the exterior walls:

1. The stud layer, either four inches thick for a 2x4 wall or six inches thick for a 2x6 wall, and
2. The masonry layer, usually six inches thick.

You may prefer to see a layer of studs (the stud zone) and a layer of masonry (brick or stone) and nothing else. No gypboard, no sheathing, no air space.

If you prefer this type of representation, it's easy to create a simplified, two-layer wall in Revit. Here's the procedure:

1. Open the floor plan view and start the Wall tool.
2. In the Properties dialog box, select Generic – 4". See figure 4.9-A.
3. In Properties, go Edit Type.
4. In Type Properties, go Duplicate …
5. Name the wall "Exterior – Masonry on 2x4 Frame."
6. Click on Structure – Edit … button.
7. In the Edit Assembly dialog box, click on Layer 1, and then click the Insert button. This adds a new row above the Core Boundary row.
8. In the new Layer 1, change the Function to Finish 1.
9. In the same row, click in the Material cell, and then click the three-dot button. The Material Browser opens.
10. In the Search box, type Brick, and in the search results, click Brick, Common. Click OK to close the Material Browser.
11. Change the Thickness in the Finish – Brick layer to six inches.
12. In Layer 3, which has the function "Structure," click in the Material cell and then click the three-dot button.
13. Search for Gyp, then from the results click on Gypsum Wall Board. Hit OK.
14. Your table should now look like figure 4.9-B.

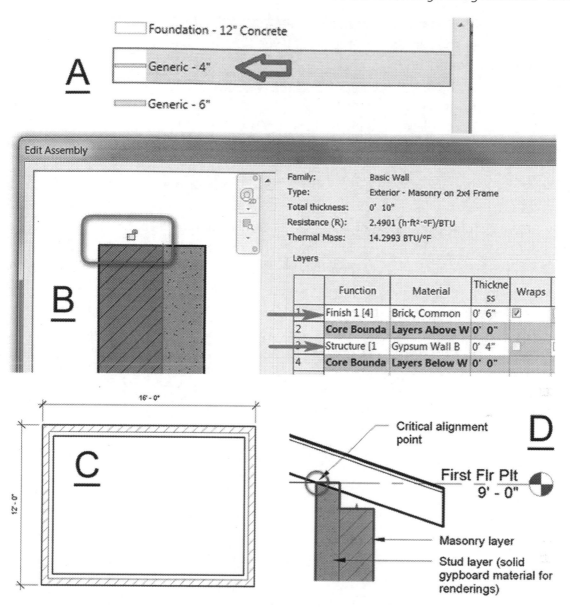

Figure 4.9. Creating a simplified, two-layer wall assembly

The reason I choose gypsum wall board for the material of the stud zone is that I want the walls in my color interior 3-D views to appear white, not the orangey color of Revit's softwood. You can choose any material you wish and adjust the cut pattern and projection pattern as desired.

You now have the wall layers, materials, and thicknesses. The next step (if desired) is to make the top of the brick layer extendible. This process was discussed earlier in this chapter, and it's similar for this simplified wall. While you're still in the Edit Assembly dialog box, follow these steps:

1. Click the Preview button.
2. Change the Preview view to Section: Modify type attributes.
3. Click on the Modify button.

4. Section View pane pan and zoom to the top of the wall. See figure 4.9-B.
5. Hover over the top edge of the brick layer. When it changes color to blue, click on it. A lock symbol appears.
6. Click on the lock symbol one time to unlock it. See figure 4.9-B.
7. It's important to exit the dialog boxes gracefully. Click on OK to close the Edit Assembly box. Click on Apply and OK to close the Type Properties box.
8. Hit OK to close the Edit Assembly box, then hit OK to close the Type Properties box.

When we apply our new two-part wall type to the floor plan, it should now look like figure 4.9-C.

The eave section using this simplified wall looks like figure 4.9-D. Note that the critical alignment point for the roof-to-wall alignment is at the interior face of the stud zone.

You can refer to my favorite exterior wall types (see figure 4.4) to see dimensions that you can use to make simplified two-layer wall types.

You now know how to create a realistic wall and how to create a simplified wall. In the next chapter, we will look at adjusting the roof's slope and rafter end shape.

Chapter 5

Roof Slope and Rafter Tail Shape

Getting into the Eave Details

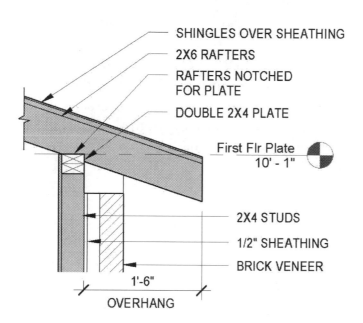

SHINGLES OVER SHEATHING

2X6 RAFTERS

RAFTERS NOTCHED FOR PLATE

DOUBLE 2X4 PLATE

First Flr Plate
10' - 1"

2X4 STUDS

1/2" SHEATHING

BRICK VENEER

1'-6"

OVERHANG

Figure 5.1. Eave detail with annotative elements added

Let's take a look at the detail eave section shown in figure 5.1. This view has some two-dimensional elements added, including leaders and detail components.

The wall is a 2x4 wood stud wall with a double 2x4 plate at the top of the stud zone. The top of the plate is aligned with the First Floor Plate level datum.

The double 2x4 plate you see here was not part of the 3-D model. It was created using 2-D Detail Components. Basic walls in Revit do not include individual studs, sole plates, or top double plates.

For more information on the graphics of this detail, see the sidebar.

Graphics Note

In the detail section to the left, I cut a section view through the model and changed the scale to 1"=1'0". I created the double 2x4 plate using the Detail Component tools. You can find these by going to Annotate tab > Detail panel > Component. I used a masking region built into the 2x4 detail component to hide the diagonal line where the rafter's bottom edge crosses through the double plate area.

The Break Line detail component is shown at the upper-left end of the roof.

To get the shading of the roof, I used an override in Visibility Graphics > Model Categories tab > Roof > Cut > Patterns column. To get the shading of the wall stud zone and gypboard, I used the Graphics settings in the Material Browser. I used the same method to get the diagonal hatch in the brick.

Controlling the Roof Slope

Now let's look at the same section without the notes and with the Properties box visible (see figure 5.2).

The roof slope is currently set at 4" to 12". This means for every twelve inches of horizontal run, the roof rises four inches vertically. See figure 5.2-A.

Due to Revit's power of *bidirectional associativity*, the Slope number in the Properties box not only displays information about the current state of the model—it can also be used to directly *modify* the model. Simply by editing the Slope number in the Properties box, you can change the actual slope of the roof in the 3-D model. Totally amazing, I would say.

To see this principle at work, change the slope setting in the Properties box to 8" / 12". Instantly, the roof in your model changes to reflect the slope setting. See figure 5.2-B.

Looking at other settings, the Roof Type (Basic roof – Wood Rafter 6" – Asphalt Shingle) is shown in the selector pane at the top. It's easy to change the roof type by opening the flyout list and selecting a different roof type—for example, a metal roof assembly.

Under Constraints, notice that the Base Level to which the roof is constrained is the First Floor Plate. There is zero offset (0'0") of the base of the roof from this Base Level. This is perfect. Ideally you will have a zero offset from the supporting wall's plate.

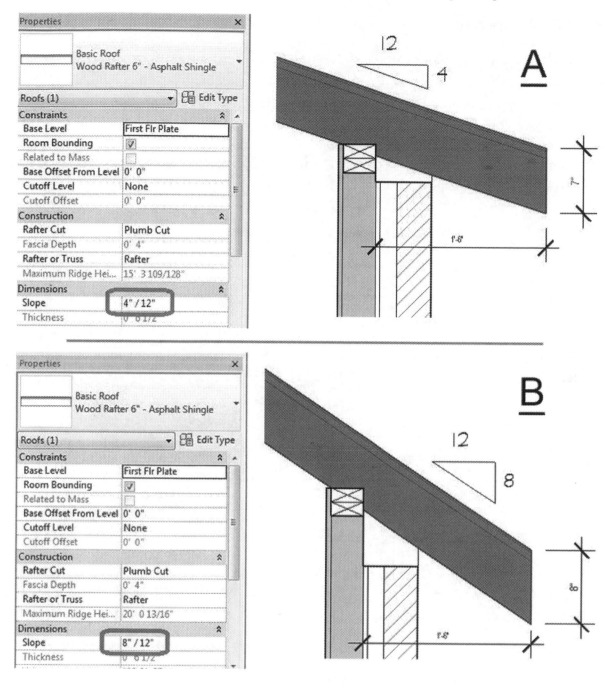

Figure 5.2. Roof slope adjusted by settings in the Properties box

Rafter Cut Options

Revit makes it easy to control the cross-section shape of the rafter ends (also known as rafter tails) at the overhangs.

If you select the roof in your model and look in the Properties dialog box under Construction, you will see a setting for Rafter Cut. This setting controls the shape of the ends of the rafters for the selected roof object.

See figure 5.3-A. Click on the current setting for Rafter Cut in the table, and you will see a down-arrow button that leads to a flyout menu with three options:

- Plumb Cut
- Two Cut – Plumb
- Two Cut – Square

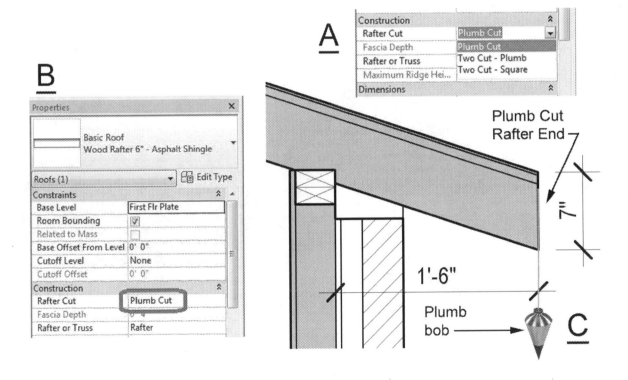

Figure 5.3. Choosing the Plumb Cut rafter shape

Let's consider the first option: Plumb Cut. If the term *plumb* is unfamiliar to you, think of a carpenter (by the name of Bob, perhaps?) using a plumb bob with a chalk-coated string to mark a perfectly vertical line for the rafter's end cut, with the rafter already in place on top of the wall. See figure 5.3-C.

Note that in this option, you cannot adjust the Fascia Depth dimension within the Properties box—it is grayed out. You get the full depth of the rafter (see figure 5.3-B). If you want a narrower fascia, you must go to the next option: Two Cut – Plumb.

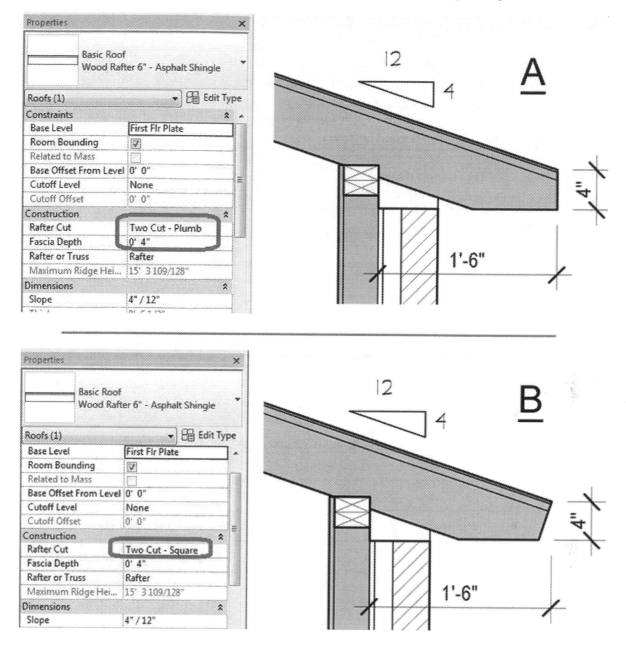

Figure 5.4. Two Cut – Plumb and Two Cut – Square rafter cut options

Changing the Rafter Cut setting to the second option Two Cut – Plumb, and choosing a relatively small Fascia Depth dimension (such as four inches), combines a true-vertical (plumb) cut with a true-horizontal cut. This option makes the rafter tail look like figure 5.4-A.

Notice that the Fascia Depth setting in the Properties box both displays and controls the four-inch dimension in the section (and, of course, the entire roof object).

Let's now look at the third option, Two Cut – Square. In this option, the word "square" does not mean "orthogonal with the designer's computer screen." Not at all. It means, "For the first cut, saw off the rafter tail at a line that's drawn exactly ninety degrees (square) to the long edge of the rafter." Think of a builder using a carpenter's square to draw the cut line at exactly ninety degrees to the top edge of the rafter, after the rafter has been installed on the wall plate.

Just as we saw in the Two Cut – Plumb option, the second cut of the "two cut" name is a true-horizontal cut, lopping off the lower corner of the overhanging rafter. Its location is controlled by the Fascia Depth setting in Properties. See figure 5.4-B.

If you're picky about precise dimensions, you should keep in mind that both the Overhang dimension and the Fascia Depth dimension are measured from the farthest edge of the top layer of the roof assembly (the "sandwich"), *not* from the end of the rafter itself.

Here's a puzzle: The Plumb Cut option is like the Two-Cut Plumb option, except that it has only one cut. Revit offers us a Two-Cut Square option. Which makes me wonder ... where is the One-Cut Square (or "Square Cut") option?

It turns out that the Two Cut – Square rafter style is really two styles in one. If you set the Fascia Depth setting to a dimension that is larger than the end of the rafter (measured vertically), the rafter tail shape becomes, in effect, "One Cut – Square," or "Square Cut." For this rafter shape, make the Fascia Depth any dimension larger than the rafter depth plus a few inches, such as 10" or 20"; it makes no difference. See figure 5.5.

This One Cut – Square style is particularly popular in rustic, mountain-lodge-style homes.

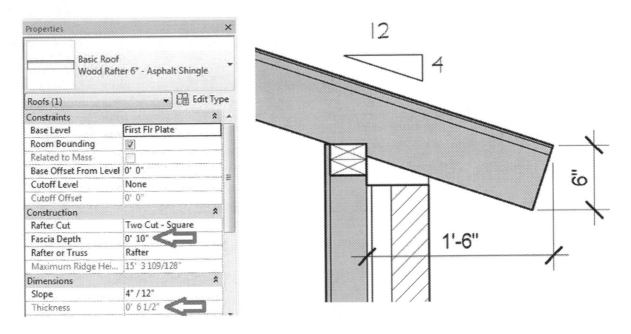

Figure 5.5. How to make a One Cut – Square rafter tail shape

Making a Thin-Overhang Roof

In some cases, you may need to have one rafter zone depth for the upper part of the roof (extending from the plate up to the ridge) but have a shallower depth in the overhanging part of the roof—the part that's visible from outside of the house.

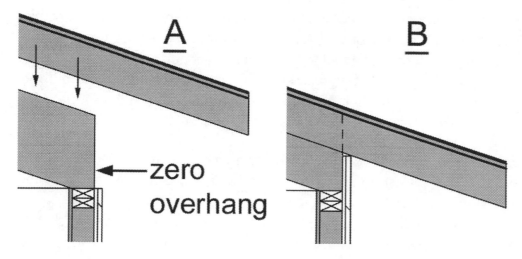

Figure 5.6. A two-depth roof

For example, let's say you are modeling a cathedral ceiling, where the ceiling layer will be attached directly to the bottom of the roof rafters. You want a twelve-inch-deep rafter zone over the interior for structural and energy conservation purposes, but you only want a six-inch-deep rafter tail at the overhang for aesthetic reasons. The top surfaces of these must align (obviously).

At the time of this writing, Revit cannot model this with a single roof object. (An item for the wishlist!) The roof I've described can be accomplished fairly easily using one of the following methods:

1. Make one twelve-inch-deep roof to rise up from the plate, with 0'0" overhang. This will make an accurate ridge height on the exterior and ceiling height inside the room. Make a separate six-inch-deep roof skirt to extend outward from the wall, forming the overhang. Align and join the two roof objects (using Geometry > Join). Or:
2. Build two roof objects over the same space, one having a twelve-inch-deep rafter zone only and no "skin" (sheathing and shingles, for example) and the other one with a six-inch-deep rafter zone and including the "skin." Extend the thinner roof outward to make the overhang while making the deeper roof's overhang 0'0". Offset the thinner roof vertically so that the top of the thinner roof's rafter zone aligns perfectly with the underside of the upper roof's sheathing.

Method 2 is the simplest, in my opinion, for most situations. Here is the step-by-step procedure (see figure 5.6):

1. Make the entire roof, including the overhang, using a 2x6" deep rafter zone.
2. Copy the roof object upward two feet or so, letting the upper roof object float in the air. You now have two roof objects, one above the other.
3. Convert the lower roof into a new roof type that has a twelve-inch-deep rafter zone and no sheathing or shingles. This roof is still anchored perfectly on the plate. Change the overhang of this lower roof to zero. See figure 5.6-A.

4. Move the upper roof object straight down until the underside of its sheathing aligns perfectly with the top of the thicker roof's rafter zone. See figure 5.6-B.
5. Use the Geometry > Join tool to join the two roof objects together.
6. Extend the finish layers of the wall assembly upward as needed to cover the exposed end of the thicker roof's rafter zone as shown. See chapter 4 (especially figure 4.8) to see how to make selected wall layers extendible.

The reason for omitting the skin in the twelve-inch-thick roof object is that two finish surfaces (such as shingles) occupying the exact same space will display in unpredictable ways in Revit.

A third method would be to create the entire roof with a twelve-inch-thick rafter zone, including the overhang, and then use a modeled-in-place void extrusion to carve away the unwanted rafter thickness in the overhanging portion of the roof. This could get very complex in three dimensions, so I don't recommend it.

You may choose method 1 if you are using Revit to do takeoffs of the rafter material. The thinner overhanging rafters could be allowed to overlap the deeper interior rafters by a few feet, just as they would in real-world construction.

Cutting Back Selected Roof Layers (In 2-D Only)

Revit allows you to pull back selected layers of the roof assembly in 2-D Section views. While this may work for Section views, it has no effect on the 3-D model or on Elevation views. Still, it may be useful in limited situations.

To make this adjustment in Section view:

1. Open a section view of the roof-to-wall connection. See figure 5.7-B.
2. Go to View tab > Graphics panel > Cut Profile button (see figure 5.7-A).
3. Hover over the roof assembly layer you want to cut back. When it's highlighted, click on it. It should now be outlined in an orange color, and you are taken to Sketch Mode.
4. Draw a new edge line where you want to cut it back to (see figure 5.7-C).
5. Verify that the small blue arrow (see figure) on the new line points to the part of the roof that you want to *keep*. If needed, click on the blue arrow to reverse its direction.
6. Click on the Big Green Checkmark. Your section should look similar to figure 5.7-D.

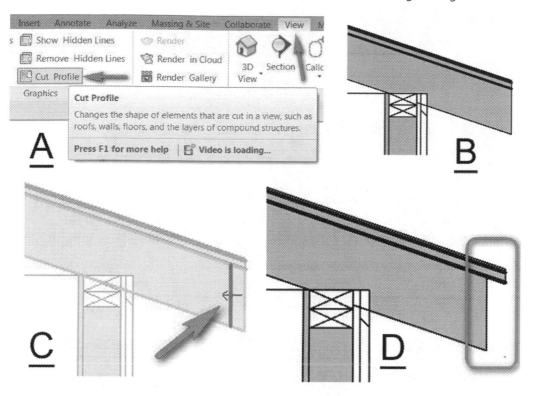

Figure 5.7. Cutting back a roof layer in Section view

Again, this only works in the active 2-D view, unfortunately. The change has no effect on the 3-D model.

Chapter 6

The Well-Connected Overhang

Overhangs in Revit are more flexible and powerful than you might expect, especially if you're coming from AutoCAD or another 2-D-based drawing software. While we discussed overhangs in the previous chapter, it's worth going into a little more depth to better understand how they work.

In any overhanging-roof design, before creating the roof, the Revit designer faces a critical decision: how best to control the overhang.

Before making a roof, decide how best to control the overhang.

I think we can agree that in the normal course of design, you can expect many changes to come along that can affect the roof-to-wall relationship, including the following:

- The wall's position may change, as when a room grows larger in plan.
- The wall type may change, say from brick veneer to stucco or siding.
- The desired length of the roof's overhang may change.
- The desired height of the eave relative to the top plate level may change.

All these can be handled easily with a well-connected overhang in Revit.

Planning Ahead When Modeling the Roof

Revit has three ways to control overhangs. The designer locks in one of these when he or she draws the roof footprint sketch. I'm listing them in order of preference, with the best method first:

Method #1:   Make the roof's footprint using the Pick Wall tool, with a preset overhang dimension measured from the *exterior face of the stud zone* (Extend to Core option).

Method #2:   Make the roof using the Pick Wall tool, with a preset overhang dimension measured from the *exterior finish face of the wall assembly* (*not* extended to core).

Method #3:   Make the roof footprint using the Draw Line tool or the Offset tool, by drawing a sketch line outside of the wall, without constraining it to the wall.

Method #1 gives the designer the most powerful and efficient control of the roof when the wall position changes. Adjustment of the roof is often done automatically with little or no cleanup by the designer. Even if the wall type changes from brick to stucco, the roof stays true to the structural wall with this option.

Method #2 also works well and updates automatically but does not adjust easily to a change from brick veneer to siding or stucco. If the modeled wall is just a generic wall, with only one amorphous layer, and is not expected to change, then this is your best choice.

Method #3 requires the most work when things change—and you know they will. It's the least desirable choice of the three.

With either Method #1 or Method #2, the roof remains anchored to the top of the supporting wall, even if the wall moves. The overhang length can be changed, if needed, just by changing the Overhang dimension in the Properties box. By adjusting the overhang in this way, the major part of the roof—the part above the plate—*does not change*. Usually this is a *huge* advantage.

Here is why I don't recommend Method #3. Method #3 creates the roof using unconstrained, free-floating footprint lines drawn in the work area. With this method, if you need to go back later and extend the roof's overhang, you have to move the roof's *slope-defining edge* outward, away from the building. The problem with this? The height of the roof's edge above the ground does not change, unless the designer changes it manually.

What *does* change is the roof's shape and position, from the eave all the way up to the peak. The designer will need to manually raise or lower the roof to return it to its proper position relative to the wall. In the process, many critical alignments in the upper part of the roof can be thrown out of kilter and may need repair. This can turn into a lot of work and wasted time, trying to manually correct the roof's position.

Whenever a roof springs upward from a supporting wall, it's to your advantage to use that wall for the roof's justification.

Making a Doghouse

To demonstrate the power of a well-modeled overhang, let's build a doghouse. Start a new project with the First Floor Plate level set at 4'0". Make four walls as shown in figure 6.1-B.

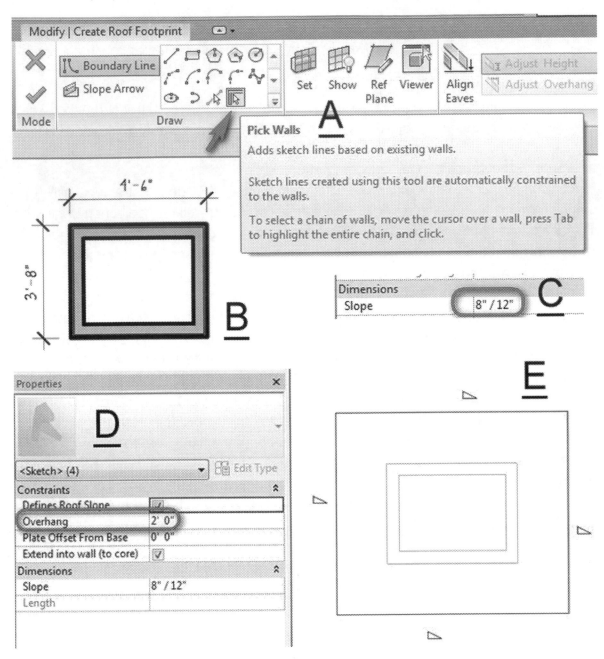

Figure 6.1. Making a doghouse roof

Now we will create a roof, with the edges of the roof's footprint justified to the walls.

Open the Roof Plan view, and make sure the Work Plane is set to First Floor Plate. Then use the Roof by Footprint tool to create a new roof.

Be sure to use the Pick Walls tool (see figure 6.1-A), with an Overhang setting of 2'0", as shown in figure 6.1-D. (You can find the Overhang setting, the Defines Slope checkbox, and the Extend into wall (to core) checkbox in either the Properties box or the Options bar.) Click on each of the walls, and you have a footprint sketch similar to figure 6.1-E.

After creating the four edges of the roof object, go to the Properties box and change the Rafter or Truss setting to Rafter. (The setting is hidden until after you create at least one edge of the roof.)

The "Rafter or Truss" option does not become available in the Properties box until after the first edge line is created in the work area.

Change the Slope setting in the Properties box to 8" / 12". See figure 6.1-C. Click on the Apply button, and then click on the Big Green Checkmark button.

Check your work by going to Section view. The results look great, as shown in figure 6.2-A. Well done!

Testing Overhang Editability

Now let's assume that a design change happens that requires us to change the overhang from 2'0" to 1'0", while keeping the roof's slope and wall plate height the same. No sweat! We do that as follows:

1. In the Roof Plan view, select the roof object and click on Edit Footprint in the ribbon.
2. Hover over any roof edge line, hit the Tab key to highlight all four edges, and click on any edge line. Voila! All four edges are selected. (This is the hover-Tab-click method of selecting all segments of a chain. It works great on either lines or walls.)
3. Change the Overhang setting in the Properties dialog box to 1'0". Click on Apply and then the Big Green Checkmark button.

The result is shown in figure 6.2-B. Note that the rafter-to-plate Critical Alignment Point (see figure 4.6) is still perfect, and the upper roof has not changed. Only the overhang length and the Plate to Eave dimension have changed. This is the way Revit prefers to handle overhangs, and once you understand how it is set up, it's very logical and reasonable.

How to Avoid the Floating Roof

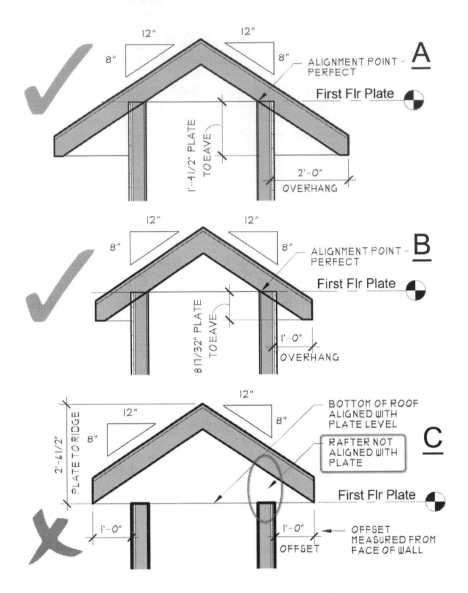

Figure 6.2. Adjusting the roof's overhang

What if, back when we were drawing the roof footprint in Sketch Mode, we used the Pick Lines tool and picked the walls' exterior faces, with a 2'0" offset dimension to create the overhang?

The Pick Lines tool, like the Lines tool, creates a line that is not justified to the wall but simply floats in space at the level of the active Work Plane. A Section view through the resulting roof is shown in figure 6.2-C.

Notice the misalignment of the rafters and the plate. The roof is floating an unknown distance above the supporting plate. Not good! Of course, we could correct this problem by lowering the roof object, but that would require several steps and some trial and error. After making that repair, the overhang can't easily be changed just by updating the overhang dimension in the property box, as in the first exercise shown in figures 6.2-A and 6.2-B. Also, if the walls move, you have another time-consuming repair job to do.

It bears repeating (pun intended): Whenever possible, it's best to justify the roof to a supporting (bearing) wall by using the Pick Walls tool to create the roof footprint. That way, you're taking advantage of Revit's intelligent editing features and saving yourself lots of time.

Justifying a Roof Object to a Beam

What if the roof you're modeling is supported not by a wall but by a beam? Unfortunately, Revit does not currently give us the capability to justify a roof to a beam in the same way that we can justify a roof to a wall. My workaround is to create the beams using a special type of wall that masquerades as a beam.

Let's say I want to make six-inch-wide by twelve-inch-deep beams around a porch, and I have created a level datum for this purpose called "Top of Porch Beams." I create a new wall type named "6" Solid Wood for Beams." Using that wall type, I model the beams around the porch, either in Roof Plan view or in Ceiling Plan view. I set both the Base Constraint and the Top Constraint of the wall/beam to be "Top of Porch Beams." Then I use a negative Base Offset setting to make the bottom of the wall/beam equal to the beam depth (in this example-12"). Next, I justify the edges of the porch roof to the wall/beam.

The downside of this workaround is that if you are linking a structural model to your architectural model, you may end up with doubled porch beams. In that case, the architectural beams will need to be hidden in all views. The upside is that the roof alignment and the overhangs work perfectly.

Chapter 7

Rafters, Trusses, and Extending to Core

Two important settings affecting the shape and size of the eave are the Rafter or Truss option, and the Overhang: Extend to Core option.

The Extend to Core option is in the Options bar and can also be found in the Properties box.

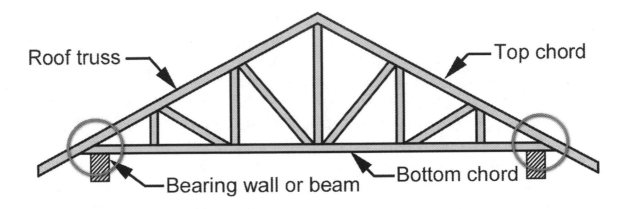

Figure 7.1. A typical wood roof truss and its supports

The Rafter or Truss option is only available in the Properties box, under the Construction heading. This option is hidden until at least one magenta-colored line is created in Sketch Mode. It remains visible and editable after the roof object is created, by selecting the roof object.

Roof trusses are sometimes used instead of the more traditional rafter construction. For a very simple roof shape, they can be more economical than rafter construction. Figure 7.1 shows a diagram of a typical roof truss. Note that the diagonal top chord member does not need to be notched to sit on the bearing wall (as in a rafter). Instead, the horizontal member (the bottom chord) of the truss sits flat on top of the bearing wall or beam. I've circled these locations.

Rafter or Truss?

This is why Revit offers two ways to justify the roof. A truss-bearing condition is very different from a rafter-bearing condition. This "Rafter or Truss" setting is only available if you use the Pick Walls tool when you create the roof.

Revit does not draw in the entire truss for you. That would be nice, right? I'll add that to my wishlist! Here's how it works. If you choose the Truss option, Revit assumes that the structural part of your roof assembly (the Core) is the top chord of an imaginary truss and adjusts the height of the top chord upward in relation to the top of the bearing wall.

The "Rafter or Truss" option is only available if you use the Pick Walls tool to create the roof.

The four-part matrix in figure 7.2 shows the different roof configurations that result from changing the Overhang Extend to Core option (Yes or No) and the Rafter or Truss option (Rafter or Truss).

The two vertical columns show the Extend to Core option switched on (left) and off (right). This controls whether the specified overhang, in this case 2'0", is measured from the exterior face of the studs (the core) or from the exterior face of the wall assembly, including any finish materials such as brick or stucco.

I like to mentally translate "Extend to" into "Measure Overhang from," which makes it a little easier to understand. If you choose not to measure the overhang from the core (unchecking the box), then Revit measures the overhang from the exterior face of the wall.

The two horizontal rows show the Rafter option (top) and the Truss option (bottom). This controls whether the roof's structural element gets notched for the wall plate as rafters typically do (top row), or flies over the plate or wall, barely touching the outside corner of the stud zone or the wall assembly, as a truss would do (bottom row).

This distinction is worth noting:

- If the Extend to Core option is checked, the roof's structural element (the roof's Core) barely touches the top-outside corner of the wall's core (i.e., the stud wall's plate).
- If Extend to Core is *not* checked, the roof's structural element barely touches the top-outside corner of the entire wall assembly (including finishes such as brick or stucco).

As discussed in chapter 4, if there are finish layers underneath the rafter zone in the roof assembly, Revit does not respect the Core Boundary layer between the rafter zone and the underside finish layer(s). It places the roof assembly's bottom-most layer—whether it's core or finish—at the alignment points shown in figure 7.2.

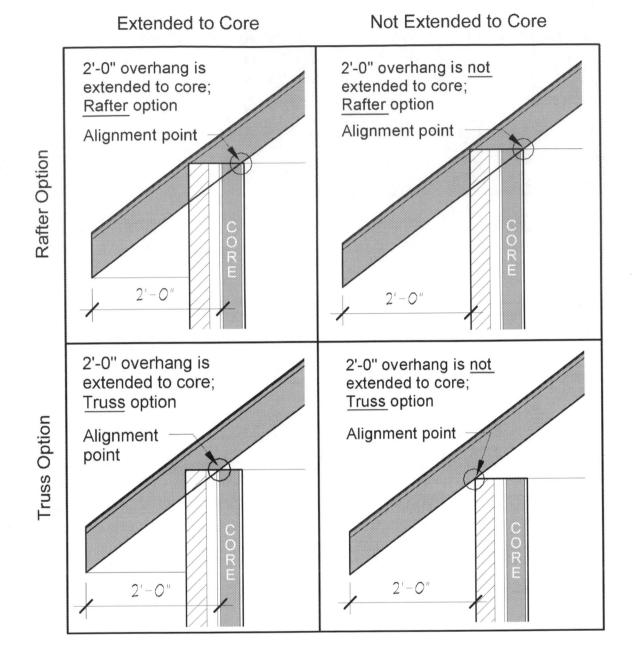

Figure 7.2. Matrix of Truss/Rafter option with Extended/Not Extended option

With this understanding, you should now be able to predict with confidence where a roof object will land on its supporting walls. This is crucial for accurate roof modeling in Revit!

Now let's see how quickly you can create a very complex, highly faceted roof using the tools we've covered.

Chapter 8

The Big, Easy, Super-Quick Roof

The Easiest Roof You'll Ever Make

Whenever you have a chain of exterior wall segments enclosing a house and all the segments have the same plate height, it's very easy to roof the house with a single hip-shaped roof object. This is one of the easiest types of roofs to make in Revit.

Let's create an example of this type of roof.

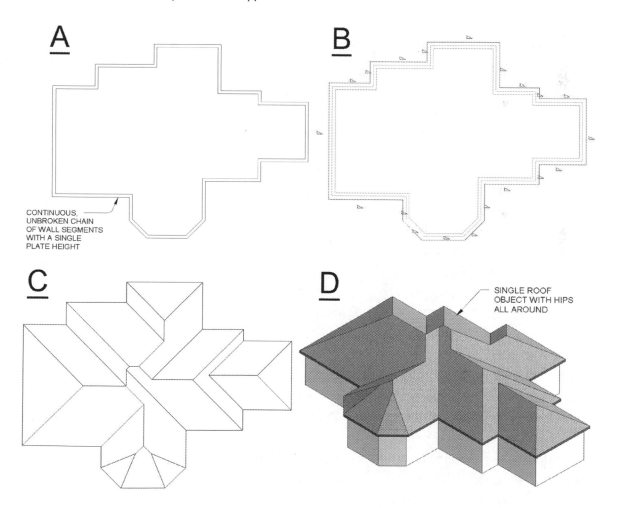

Figure 8.1. Creating a very complex yet very quick and easy roof

Here are the steps.

Start a new RVT project file using your custom residential template RTE file (see chapter 2 for how to make a custom template). Open the First Floor plan view.

Create the Walls (Allow Sixty Seconds)

Start the Wall tool (Architecture tab > Build panel > Wall) and set the Top Constraint in the Properties box to Up to Level: First Floor Plate. Just keep the default wall type (Generic) in the selector pane.

Draw a chain of walls around the imaginary house. Each segment should be approximately the length of one or two rooms (maybe 8' to 24' long), making generally a house-type shape, using mostly ninety-degree or forty-five-degree corners. Return to the starting point and be sure to close the loop of wall segments. The shape of the plan can be just about any shape imaginable, with as many corners as you want. See an example in figure 8.1-A.

Create the Roof (Allow Sixty Seconds)

Now create the roof.

1. Double-click on the Roof Plan in the Project Browser. In the ribbon, go to Architecture tab> Build panel > Roof by Footprint. You are now in Sketch Mode.
2. Keep all the defaults in the Options bar as they are: the Defines Slope option checked, the Overhang distance set to 1'0", and the Extend to Wall Core option unchecked.
3. Select one of the Shingle Roof types in the Selection Pane of the Properties dialog box.
4. Keep the slope of the roof at the default value, which is 9" / 12".
5. Set the Base Level in the Properties box to First Floor Plate.
6. Using the Pick Walls tool, click on each of the wall segments, following a clockwise path. No trimming necessary! See figure 8.1-B.
7. Hit the Big Green Checkmark button in the ribbon.

The roof plan should now look something like figure 8.1-C.

Open the Default 3-D view (I usually click the Doghouse button in the Quick Access Toolbar). Change the Visual Style (the button is at the bottom left of your work area, near the scale selector) to be Realistic. Your Default 3-D view should now look something like figure 8.1-D.

It's hard to imagine roof creation being much quicker or easier than that. Imagine the time required to construct a 2-D roof plan, 3-D perspective, and elevations of a house like this using CAD or (groan) a pencil!

Once the walls are in place, with a little practice, this type of roof can be modeled in minutes. And you now have not only a roof plan but a 3-D model ready for use in perspectives, elevations, sections, takeoffs, and more.

Best of all, if you decide to change the location of a wall in a plan, you can simply move the wall, and the roof adjusts instantly. Let's say, for example, a living room wall needs to move two feet outward in the floor plan. Instantly, the roof object responds and reconfigures itself, keeping the desired overhang and slope. The hips and valleys automatically adjust to accommodate the change. All the plans and other views in Revit are automatically updated before you can even think about it. Very cool!

We will learn how to dress up this roof with soffits, fasciae, and gutters in a later chapter. Now let's look at some of the cool roof shapes you can make with Revit.

Chapter 9

The Revit Roof-Modeling Toolbox

Learning Revit's Roof-Making Tools

Revit offers three tools specifically designed for making roof objects. See figure 9.1-A. They are

1.   Roof by Footprint,
2.   Roof by Extrusion, and
3.   Roof by Face.

Generally we will use the Roof by Footprint tool whenever we can, since that tool is the easiest and simplest to use. If that doesn't do the job, next we will look to the Roof by Extrusion tool. If that doesn't fit the bill, we will consider the Roof by Face tool, which is usually the most time-consuming of the three options.

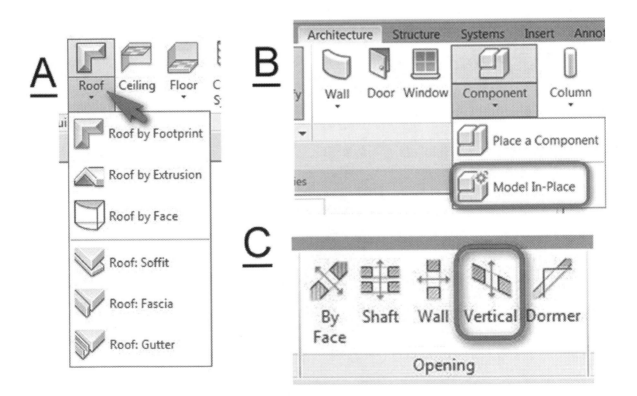

Figure 9.1. Various tools Revit provides for shaping roofs

Another option is to create an In-Place Family using the solid modeling tools and put it in the Roofs category. See figure 9.1-B.

You could even create a roof family in the Family Editor as an (RFA) file. Usually that's not the preferred method, because you do not have the walls or the nearby roofs available to snap or measure to. In certain cases, such as the creation of an ornate dormer, it might make sense to do it this way.

Additive vs. Subtractive Tools

In addition to the "additive" form-building tools discussed above, Revit also offers "subtractive" *form-removing* tools that make roof creation much simpler. Among these are the Opening tools. See figure 9.1-C.

One great subtractive tool that Revit offers is the Vertical Opening tool. You can find this tool in the ribbon in the Architecture tab > Opening panel > Vertical button. This tool is useful not just for making openings, such as a hole in a roof, but also for custom-shaping the ends of a roof object, for example where it meets another roof object at a hip.

Another useful tool is the Dormer Opening tool. This tool cuts an opening for a dormer, once the dormer has been modeled. We will discuss dormers in a later chapter.

Yet another subtractive tool that can be used to cut material away from roofs is the Model In-Place tool. You can use this tool to create a void extrusion, which can then be used to cut material away from a roof object using the Geometry Cut tool. This will be discussed in a later chapter in the procedure for making a Winged Gable roof.

One major advantage to using subtractive tools such as Vertical Opening and Void Form is that they have no effect on the shape of the roof other than simply removing part of it. Often when you try to remove part of a roof by changing the footprint, it affects other parts of the roof in unexpected ways. I've learned to use the subtractive tools liberally.

Additional Tools

Figure 9.2 is a handy table showing roof slope ratios and their equivalent angles of slope in degrees. This table will be useful in some of the exercises that follow.

Roof Slope Ratios, Angles & Multipliers

Slope Ratio h w	Degrees	h/w	w/h	Slope Ratio h w	Degrees	h/w	w/h
1 " / 12 " =	4.76	0.08	12.00	11 " / 12 " =	42.51	0.92	1.09
2 " / 12 " =	9.46	0.17	6.00	12 " / 12 " =	45	1.00	1.00
3 " / 12 " =	14.04	0.25	4.00	13 " / 12 " =	47.29	1.08	0.92
4 " / 12 " =	18.43	0.33	3.00	14 " / 12 " =	49.40	1.17	0.86
5 " / 12 " =	22.62	0.42	2.40	15 " / 12 " =	51.34	1.25	0.80
6 " / 12 " =	26.57	0.50	2.00	16 " / 12 " =	53.13	1.33	0.75
7 " / 12 " =	30.26	0.58	1.71	17 " / 12 " =	54.78	1.42	0.71
8 " / 12 " =	33.69	0.67	1.50	18 " / 12 " =	56.31	1.50	0.67
9 " / 12 " =	36.87	0.75	1.33	24 " / 12 " =	63.43	2.00	0.50
10 " / 12 " =	39.81	0.83	1.20	30 " / 12 " =	68.20	2.50	0.40

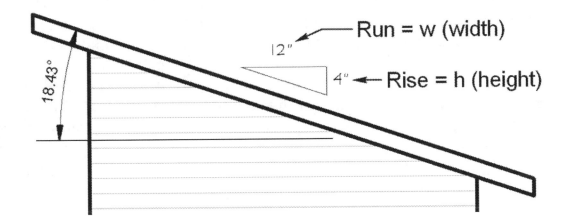

Figure 9.2. Roof Slope Ratios, Angles, and Multipliers table with an example diagram

The height/width and width/height factors in figure 9.3 can be used as multipliers to calculate how far a roof will rise in a given run, or vice versa.

For example, if a roof has a slope of 7" / 12", and its horizontal run is 8 feet, how much will it rise in that distance?

Solution: Convert 8 feet to 96 inches. On figure 9.3, find the row for 7" / 12" slope. Since the roof is less than 12" / 12", we know that the rise will be less than the run. The h/w column shows a multiplier of 0.58. Multiplying 96" x 0.58, we get 55.68" total rise. Next we will convert the decimal component to a fraction. Multiplying 0.68 x 16, we get 0.39, which we round up to 4, and this is the number of sixteenths of an inch. So the total rise is 55 4/16", or 55 1/4". Don't you just love fractions?

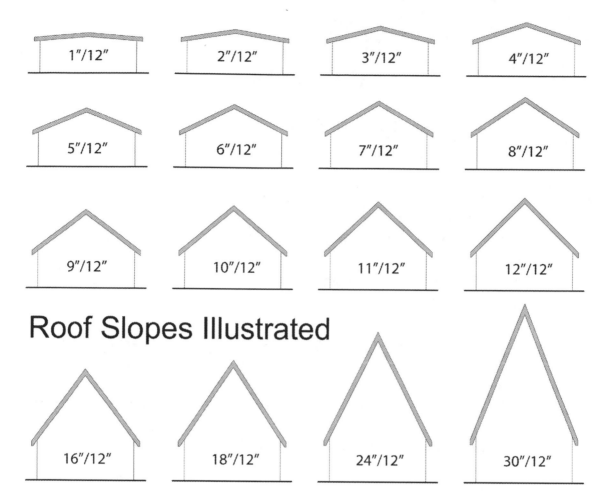

Figure 9.3. Various roof slope ratios shown in elevation

Figure 9.3 is a table of various roof slopes in elevation. It can help you get a feel for the slope ratio numbers in terms of their visual effect. A 12" / 12" slope equals forty-five degrees, a familiar number.

Generally, it is a good idea to avoid specifying wood or composition shingles on roofs having a slope of 3" / 12" or less. For roofs with less than 3" / 12" slope, a standing-seam metal roof, a built-up roof, or a membrane roof will be better options.

We have now built a good foundation for understanding the tools that Revit gives us to create realistic, buildable roofs.

In the next chapter, we will present a gallery of basic roof shapes and follow that with exercises describing the steps used to model each shape.

Chapter 10

Basic Roof Shapes Gallery

I've assembled a collection of basic roof shapes, shown in figure 10.1. I think of these shapes as the building blocks of residential roofs. These basic shapes can be created easily in Revit. They can stand alone, or they can be combined to make more complex roofs. In the next sixteen chapters, we'll discuss how to model each basic roof shape individually.

In the gallery, you will see that the simplest roofs have only one or two planar faces. The more complex roofs have four to eight faces, and then there are the conical, domed, and segmented roofs, which have both simple and complex curves.

While this is not an exhaustive list of roof shapes, I believe that these sixteen basic shapes provide a good representation of the roof shapes that are used in most residences, either alone or in combination.

A suitable-for-framing, high-quality printed poster of the Roof Shapes Gallery can be yours by visiting www.BestCADtips.com/poster. Perfect for displaying on your office wall!

After the gallery, we will start with the simplest roof shape, the shed roof, and progress to the more complex shapes. For each shape, we will describe the procedure for modeling the roof.

The procedures that accompany each roof shape assume that you are using the RTE template file that we created in chapter 2.

Use your template file from chapter 2 for the procedures.

Since there are quite a few roof shapes shown in the gallery, I've divided them into the four groups below. Figure 10.2 shows the grouping of the roof shapes.

The detailed studies of the roof shapes will be organized as follows:

•	Chapters 11–14	Group A	Simple Rectangular Roofs
•	Chapters 15–18	Group B	Intermediate Rectangular Roofs
•	Chapters 19–22	Group C	Complex Rectangular Roofs
•	Chapters 23–26	Group D	Circular and Polygonal Roofs

A Gallery of Basic Roof Shapes

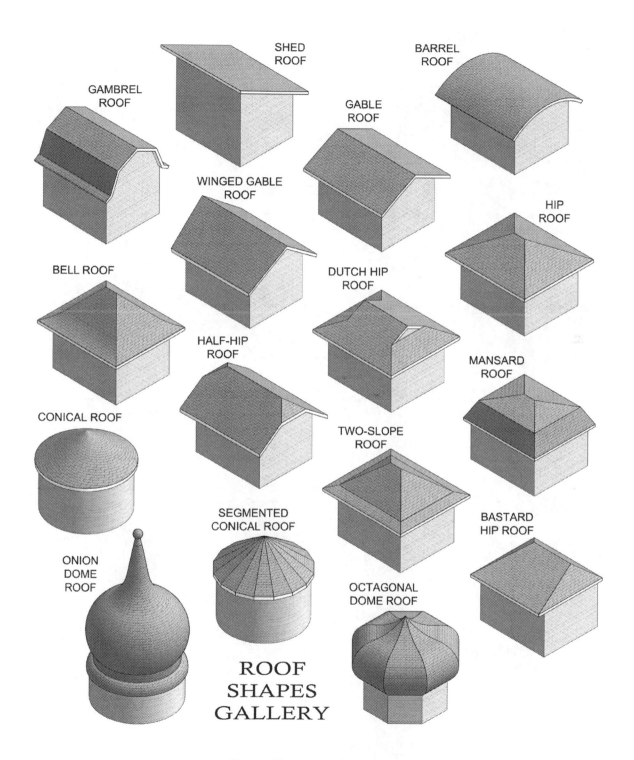

Figure 10.1. A gallery of basic roof shapes modeled in Revit

Mark S. Sadler, RA, NCARB

Gallery of Roof Shapes Showing Groups

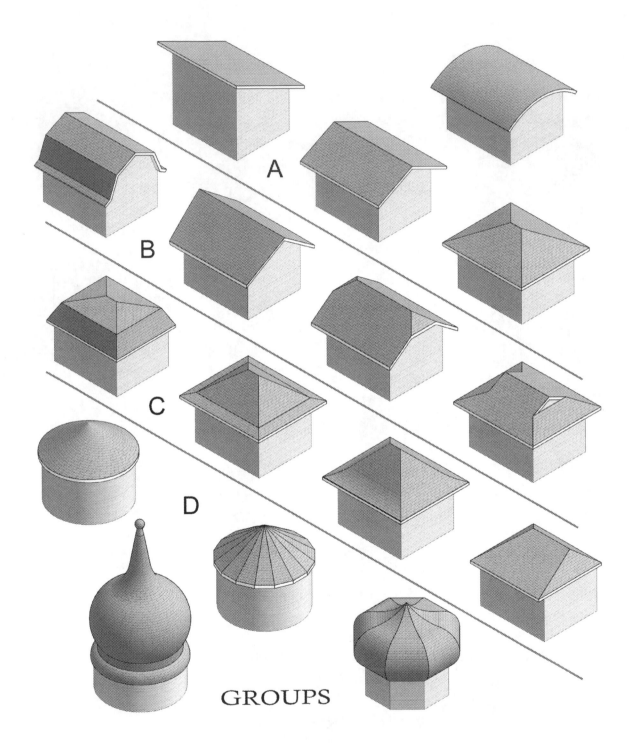

Figure 10.2. Grouping of the roof types for the following chapters

Group A: Simple Rectangular Roofs

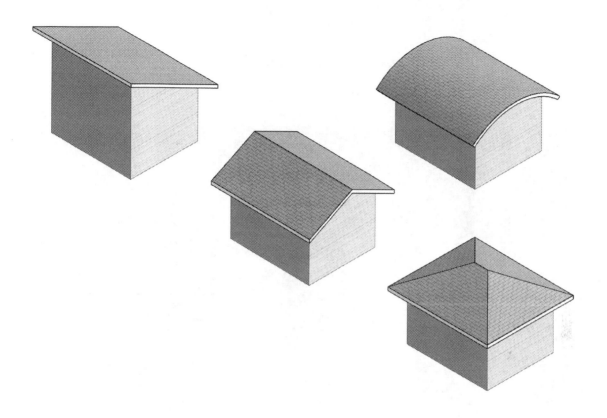

The Shed Roof   •   The Barrel Roof

The Gable Roof

The Hip Roof

Chapter 11

Modeling the Shed Roof

Figure 11.1. A shed roof used to make a dramatic element in a contemporary-styled house

Other than a truly flat roof, the simplest of all the roof shapes is the shed roof. Sometimes referred to as a mono-pitched roof, the shed roof has only one slope-defining edge and only one roof face. The shed roof can be very dramatic due to its simplicity.

After creating the roof, the walls generally need to be extended up to the roof. Revit has a great tool to accomplish this. It's called Attach Top/Base.

After the walls are attached to the roof, they will stay attached to it, regardless of any changes you make to the height or slope of the roof.

Procedure for Creating a Shed Roof

1. Prepare four supporting walls, with the top constraints of the walls set to "First Floor Plate." The plan view dimensions of the walls in this example are twenty feet by fifteen feet.
2. In Roof Plan view, set the work plane to Level: First Floor Plate (go to Architecture tab > Work Plane panel > Set).
3. Click on the Roof by Footprint tool.
4. Verify that the Roof Type you want is shown in the Selection Pane of the Properties dialog box.
5. In the Options bar:
   a. Set the desired Overhang distance in the Options bar (this example uses 2'0").
   b. Check the Extend to wall core option in the Options bar.
   c. Ensure that the Defines Slope option is checked in the Options bar.

6. Using the Pick Walls tool, click on the wall that will support the slope-defining edge, making sure that the overhang preview line is outside of the building.
7. Set the desired slope (this example uses 6" / 12") for the Slope Defining Edge in the Properties box (under Dimensions heading) and hit Apply. As an alternate, you can go to the work area and click on the slope ratio text (which defaults to 9" / 12") next to the magenta triangle icon. Once you're in text editing mode, just type 6 [ENTER]. Revit converts the entry to 6" / 12".
8. In the Options bar, deselect the Slope Defining option.
9. Using the Pick Walls tool, click on the other three walls, again making sure that the overhang preview line is outside of the building.
10. Select Rafter for the Rafter or Truss option in Properties box (under Construction heading).

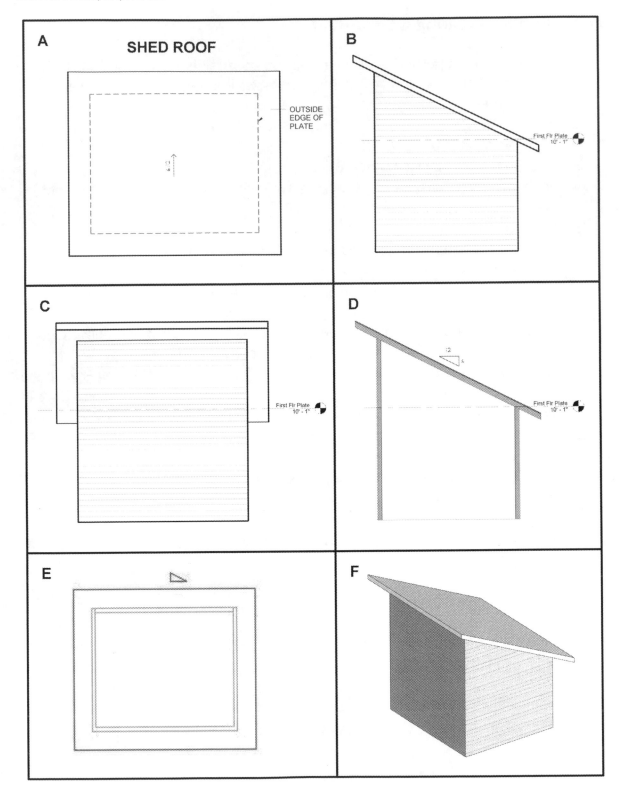

Figure 11.2. Six views of a shed roof building

11. Check the sketch to ensure proper corner connections and slope definitions, and then click the Big Green Checkmark button in the ribbon to accept the sketch and create the 3-D roof.

The only remaining step is attaching the walls to the roof. See figure 3.4 in chapter 3. Go to the default 3-D view. Select a wall that does not reach to the roof. Attach the top of the wall to the roof as follows: Go to Modify | Walls tab > Modify Wall panel > Attach Top/ Base. Click on the linework of the roof. The wall is now attached to the roof object. If the roof object is moved or changed, the wall will remain attached.

Repeat as needed for the other walls. Done!

Chapter 12

Modeling the Gable Roof

Figure 12.1. A traditional house with intersecting gable roofs

The gable roof is similar to the shed roof, except that two edges (on opposite sides) are slope defining. There are two roof faces making up a gable roof.

The word "gable" technically refers to the triangular area enclosed by the inverted V shape of the roof at the end of the building. This triangular area may be expressed architecturally, or not.

The gable roof shape is very popular and may be the most-used roof shape of all time for houses. It tends to have a lower peak height than a shed roof, given an equal covered area, and is easy to build. It has a strong linear quality.

The gable roof is easily modeled in Revit.

Procedure for Creating a Gable Roof

1. Prepare four supporting walls, with the top constraints of the walls set to "First Floor Plate." The plan view dimensions of the building in this example are twenty feet by fifteen feet.
2. In Roof Plan view, set the work plane to Level: First Floor Plate (go to Architecture tab > Work Plane panel > Set).
3. Click on the Roof by Footprint tool.
4. Verify that the Roof Type you want is shown in the Selection Pane of the Properties dialog box.
5. In the Options bar:
    a. Set the desired Overhang distance in the Options bar (this example uses 2'0").
    b. Check the Extend to wall core option in the Options bar.
    c. Ensure that the Defines Slope option is checked in the Options bar.

6. Using the Pick Walls tool, click on two opposite walls that will support the slope-defining edges, making sure that the overhang preview line is outside of the building.
7. Select the two slope-defining edges. Set the desired slope for the two Slope Defining Edges in the Properties box, under the Dimensions heading. This example uses 6"/12". Hit Apply.
8. In the Options bar, deselect the Slope Defining option.
9. Using the Pick Walls tool, click on the other two walls, again making sure that the overhang preview line is outside of the building.
10. Check the sketch to ensure proper corner connections and slope definitions, then click the Big Green Checkmark button in the ribbon to accept the sketch and create the 3-D roof.
11. With the roof still selected, choose Rafter in the Rafter or Truss option in Properties box (under Construction heading).
12. Go to the Section view to verify that the roof and walls are meeting properly. See figure 12.2-D.

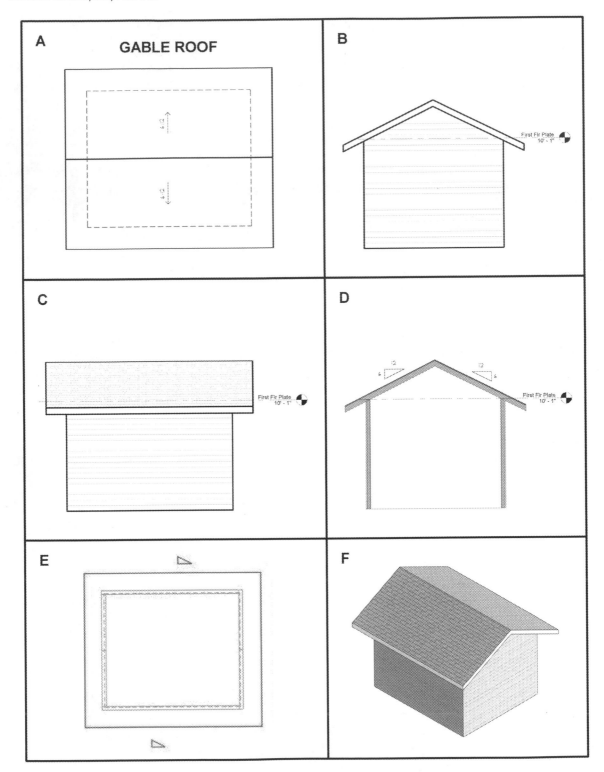

Figure 12.2. Six views of a gable roof building

13. Go to 3-D view. Select an end wall that does not extend to the roof. Attach the top of the wall to the roof. Go to Modify | Walls tab > Modify Wall panel > Attach Top/ Base. Repeat for the other end wall.

Chapter 13

Modeling the Hip Roof

Figure 13.1. A traditional hip roof house

The hip roof is similar to the gable roof, except that all four of the edges of the roof are slope defining. The hip roof on a simple rectangular building has four roof faces. The roof faces, and therefore the roof as a whole, tend to be somewhat concealed or minimized when viewed from the street.

The hip roof often has gutters on all four sides. This makes the gutters and downspouts a major visual element in the house's appearance. It's a good idea to have your Revit family library stocked with your favorite gutters, collector boxes, and downspouts.

Procedure for Creating a Hip Roof

1. Prepare four supporting walls, with the top constraints of the walls set to "First Floor Plate." The plan view dimensions of the building in this example are twenty feet by fifteen feet.
2. In Roof Plan view, set the work plane to Level: First Floor Plate (go to Architecture tab > Work Plane panel > Set).
3. Click on the Roof by Footprint tool.
4. Verify that the Roof Type you want is shown in the Selection Pane of the Properties dialog box.
5. In the Options bar:
   a. Set the desired Overhang distance in the Options bar (this example uses 2'0").
   b. Check the Extend to wall core option in the Options bar.
   c. Ensure that the Defines Slope option is checked in the Options bar.

6. Using the Pick Walls tool, click on all four walls, moving in a clockwise direction, making sure that the overhang preview line is outside of the building. Hit the Escape key twice to exit the Pick Walls tool.
7. Set the desired slope for all four of the edges in the Properties box (under Dimensions heading). This example uses 6"/12". Hit the Apply button.
8. Check the sketch to ensure proper corner connections and slope definitions, then click the Big Green Checkmark button in the ribbon to accept the sketch and create the 3-D roof.
9. With the roof still selected, choose Rafter in the Rafter or Truss option in Properties box (under Construction heading). Hit the Apply button.
10. Go to the section view to verify that the roof and walls are meeting properly. See figure 13.2-D.

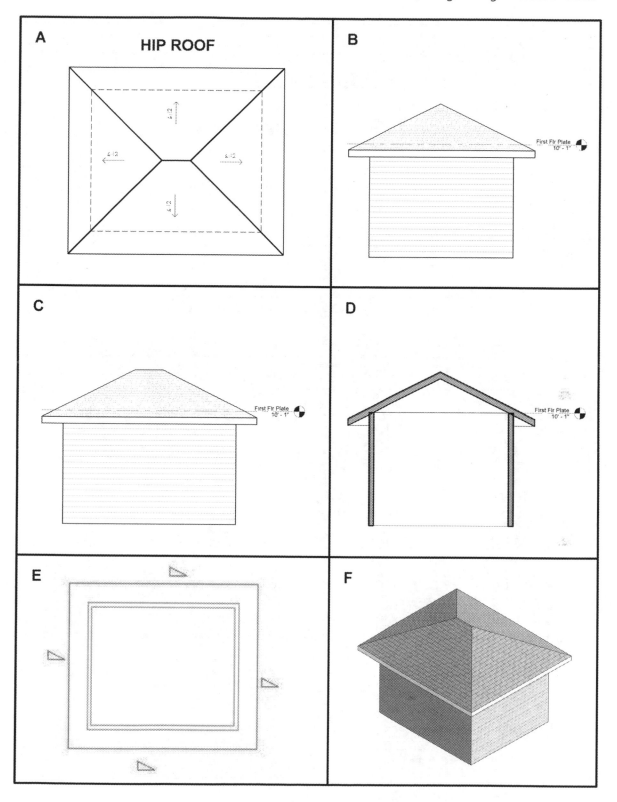

Figure 13.2. Six views of a hip roof building

Chapter 14

Modeling the Barrel Roof

Figure 14.1. Three barrel roofs form a symmetrical composition in this house

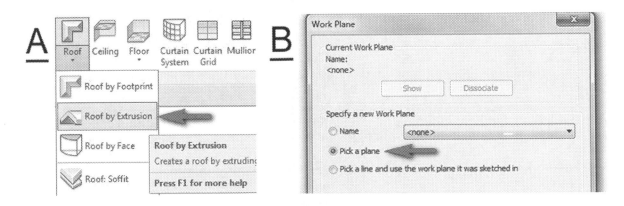

Figure 14.2. Starting to create a Roof by Extrusion

The barrel roof resembles part of a barrel sliced vertically and turned on its side. It requires bending the roofing substrate material and surface material. Since it has an area on top that is nearly true level, it is usually covered with metal roofing panels to prevent leaking.

The barrel roof can have a dramatic, graceful appearance. Unlike the roof shapes we have studied so far, this one requires the use of the Roof by Extrusion tool. It is designed in Elevation view rather than in Plan view.

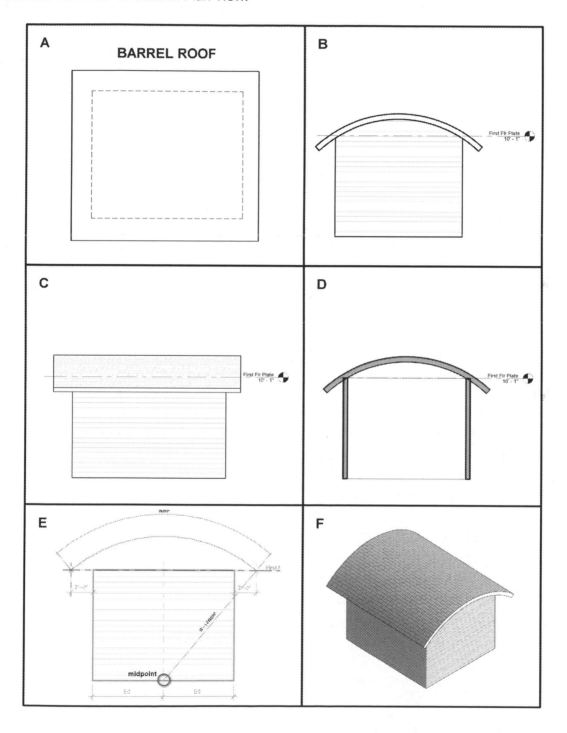

Figure 14.3. Six views of the barrel roof building

Procedure for Creating a Barrel Roof

1. Prepare four supporting walls, with the tops of the walls justified to a level called "First Floor Plate." The plan view dimensions of the building in this example are twenty feet by fifteen feet.

2. In the End Elevation view, draw two vertical drafting lines crossing the plate level line. Locate each line 2'0" horizontally away from the wall, with one on each side. See figure 14.4-C.

3. While still in elevation view, click on the Roof by Extrusion tool. It's in Architecture tab > Build panel > Roof flyout menu > Roof by Extrusion. See figure 14.2-A.

4. In the Work Plane dialog box, verify that the "Pick a plane" radio button is selected (see figure 14.2-B). Click OK to close the box and prepare to pick the work plane in the work.

5. In the Elevation view, hover over the end wall of the building. Watch for a blue outline to appear around the end wall. A tooltip saying "Walls: Basic Wall Exterior etc." should appear. Click on the wall to designate the face of the wall as the current Work Plane.

6. The Roof Reference Level and Offset dialog box will appear (see figure 14.4-A). For the level, select First Floor Plate. Leave the offset at zero. Click on OK. This ties your roof to the selected level. If that level changes height, your roof will move with it.

7. Now you are in Sketch Mode. In the Draw panel, click on the Center-ends Arc tool. See figure 14.4-B.

8. For the center point, click on the midpoint of the bottom edge of the wall. Draw the arc in a counterclockwise direction between the reference lines. See figure 14.4-C.

9. In the Properties box:
   a. Verify that the Roof Type you want is shown in the Selection Pane of the Properties dialog box.
   b. Set the Extrusion Start value at 2'0". This positive value is measured toward the viewer from the current Work Plane.
   c. Set the Extrusion End value at-17'0". This negative value is measured away from the viewer from the current work plane.

10. Click the Big Green Checkmark button to accept the sketch and create the 3-D roof.

11. The roof may be located a bit too high. Go to the Section view (see figure 14.3-D) and use the "Nudge" tool—the four arrow keys on your keyboard—to lower the roof downward into its proper position.

12. Go to the Side Elevation view to adjust the ends of the extrusion, using the blue shape handles. If you're only looking for a quick-and-dirty length adjustment, you can do that in the Default 3-D view. For higher precision, set up reference planes in the side elevation and snap the roof extrusion ends to the reference planes.

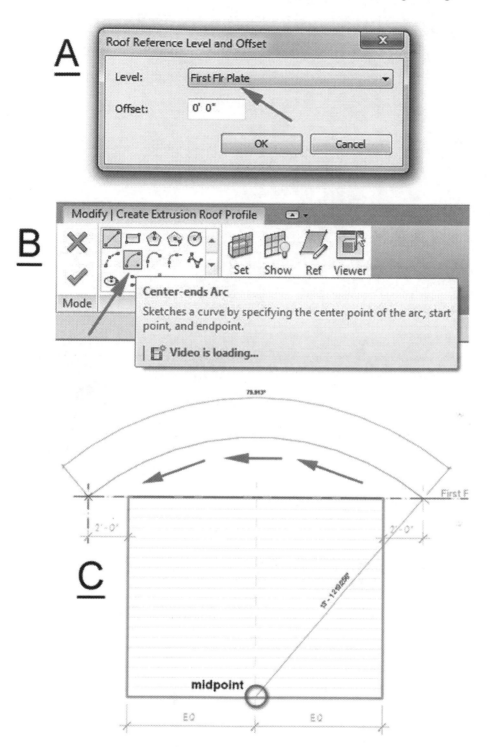

Figure 14.4. Creating a Roof by Extrusion in Sketch Mode

Group B: Intermediate Rectangular Roofs

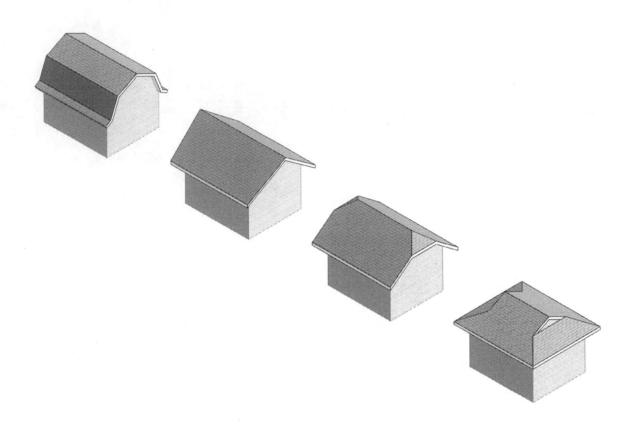

The Gambrel Roof

The Winged Gable Roof

The Half-Hip Roof

The Dutch Hip Roof

Chapter 15

Modeling the Gambrel Roof

Figure 15.1. A traditional gambrel house

There is something irresistibly charming about the gambrel roof shape. It conjures up timeless associations with farms, barns, livestock, harvest, and the good life in the country.

It is also a very practical shape for a house, with lots of second-floor or third-floor living space inside its steeply sloped roof planes.

There are a number of possible methods of modeling the gambrel shape in Revit. I usually model the gambrel roof as an extrusion, similar to the barrel roof. The difference is that instead of sketching an arc shape, you sketch a segmented line shape.

Procedure for Creating a Gambrel Roof

1. Prepare four supporting walls, with the tops of the walls justified to a level called "First Floor Plate." The Plan view dimensions of the building in this example are twenty feet by fifteen feet.

2. Go to Elevation view, click on the Roof by Extrusion tool. You'll find it by going to Architecture tab > Build panel > Roof flyout menu > Roof by Extrusion.

3. In the Work Plane dialog box, verify that the "Pick a plane" radio button is selected (see figure 15.2-A). Click OK to close the box and go to the work area to pick the work plane.

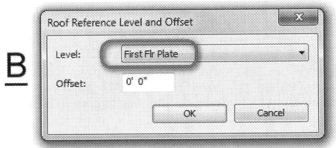

Figure 15.2. The Work Plane dialog box

4. In the Elevation view, hover over the end wall of the building. Watch for a blue outline to appear around the end wall. A tooltip saying "Walls: Basic Wall Exterior etc." should appear. Click on the wall to select the face of the wall to be the current Work Plane.

5. The Roof Reference Level and Offset dialog box will appear. See figure 15.2-B. For the level, select First Floor Plate. Leave the offset at zero. Click on OK. This setting specifies the level that the roof is justified to. If this level moves up or down in the future, the roof will move with it.

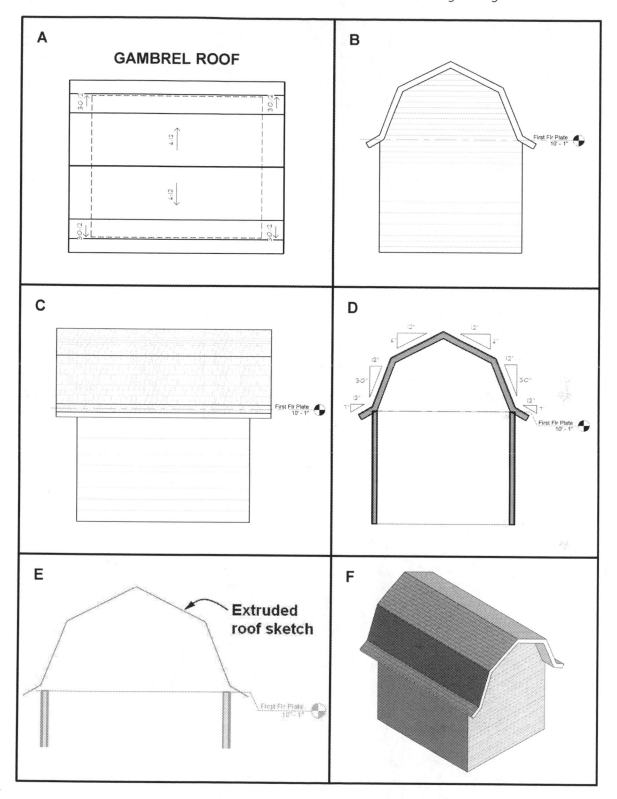

Figure 15.3. Six views of the gambrel roof

6. Now you are in Sketch Mode. In the Draw panel, verify that the Line tool is selected. Draw lines as shown in figure 15.3-E. If you wish, you can use the dimensions in figure 15.4 as a guide. Notice the various slope ratios shown in this elevation. You can convert these slope ratios into decimal degrees using the Slope Ratio conversion table provided in chapter 9, figure 9.2.

7. In the Properties box:
   a. Verify that the Roof Type you want is shown in the Selection Pane of the Properties dialog box.
   b. Set the Extrusion Start value at 2'0". This positive value is measured *toward* the viewer from the work plane.
   c. Set the Extrusion End value at-17'0". This negative value is measured *away from* the viewer from the work plane.

8. Click the Big Green Checkmark button in the ribbon to accept the sketch and create the 3-D roof.

9. The roof may be placed a bit too high or low. Go to the Section view and use the "Nudge" arrow keys to nudge the roof up or down into its proper position.

10. Go to the Side Elevation view to adjust the ends of the extrusion as needed, using the blue shape handles and aligning to reference planes or drafting lines as needed.

11. In the 3-D view, use the Attach Top/Base tool to extend the end walls up to the roof.

Done! Your roof should look something like figure 15.3-F.

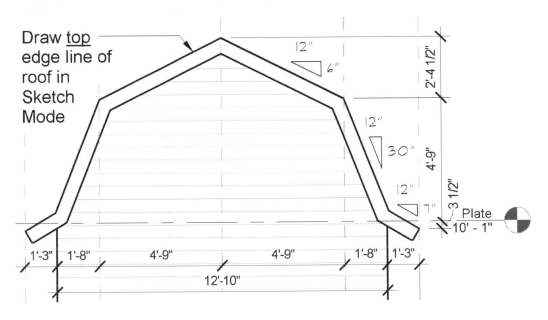

Figure 15.4. Creating a gambrel roof extrusion

Chapter 16

Modeling the Winged Gable Roof

Figure 16.1. A winged gable roof house

The winged gable roof is similar to the gable roof. The difference is that its ends are terminated at an oblique angle as viewed in side elevation, with the end of the ridge extending farther than the ends of the eaves. This roof shape was used in many of the great architect Frank Lloyd Wright's houses.

The best way I've found to model this roof shape is to create a gable roof that extends a few feet beyond the end wall of the house and then create a *void extrusion* and use it to cut off the end of the gable roof at the desired angle.

The angle of cut in the example below is nine degrees off of vertical. On larger roofs, an angle as small as two degrees might give the desired effect.

Of course, one could simply edit the footprint of the roof in plan to create this shape. One of the advantages of the void extrusion method shown below is that, once you choose an angle for the cutoff, you can use it consistently in all the roofs of a project, regardless of the roof's size and slope. No calculations required. Also, the void extrusion method gives you a better roof silhouette, with no unsightly joint line at the top where the two fasciae meet.

Procedure for Creating a Winged Gable Roof

1. Follow all the steps for making a gable roof listed in chapter 12, except this time make the overhangs at the east and west ends of the roof (the non-slope-defining edges) extend 3'0" beyond the building walls. The other overhangs can stay at 2'0".

2. In Side Elevation view (see figure 16.3-C), go to Architecture tab > Build panel > Component flyout menu and click on the Model In-Place button. See figure 16.2-A.

3. In the Family Category and Parameters dialog box, choose Roofs. See figure 16.2-B.

4. In the Name dialog box, enter the name "Void 01." Click on OK.

5. Go to Create tab > Forms panel > Void Forms flyout menu and click on Void Extrusion. See figure 16.2-C.

6. In the Work Plane dialog box, verify that the radio button for "Pick a plane" is selected, and hit OK. Next you will pick the plane.

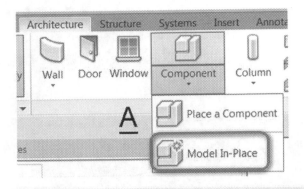

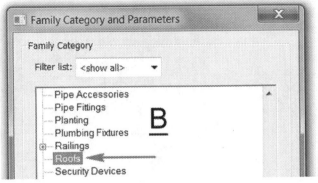

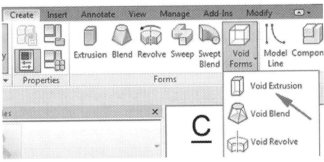

Figure 16.2. Making a void extrusion

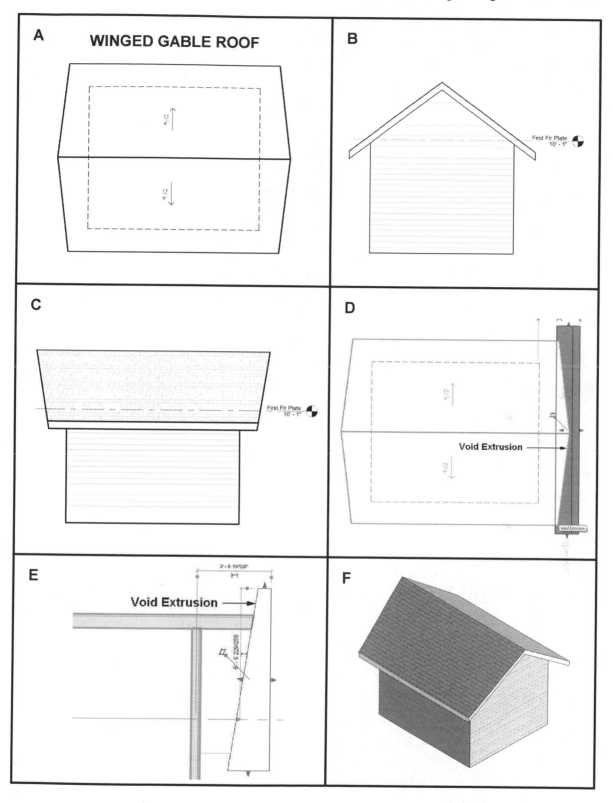

Figure 16.3. Six views of the winged gable roof

7. Hover over the side wall of the house. A blue line will appear around three sides of the wall, and a tooltip box will appear saying "Walls: Basic wall etc." Click on the wall to set the work plane.

8. The active tab in the ribbon should say "Modify | Create Void Extrusion," and you are in Sketch Mode. The Line tool should be selected in the green-colored Draw panel.

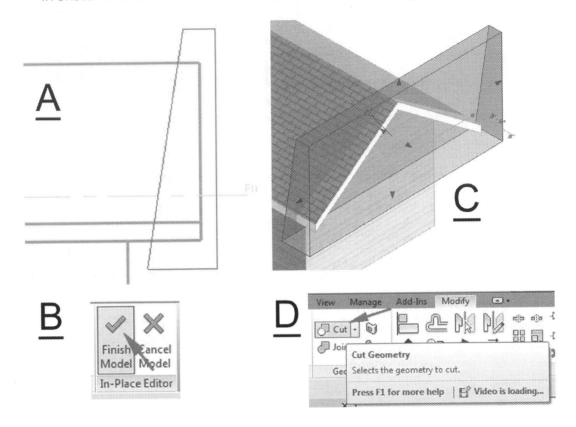

Figure 16.4. Void extrusion created

9. Using the Line tool, draw a shape similar to that shown in figure 16.4-A. Create the slanting line by making a vertical line and then using the Rotate tool to rotate the line by negative nine degrees. Draw the top and bottom lines staying a short distance above and below the roof object as shown. The true-vertical line on the right side should be at least a foot away from the end of the gable roof. Trim the corners as needed.

10. In the Properties box:
    a. Set the Extrusion Start value at 17'0". This positive value is measured *away from* the viewer from the work plane.
    b. Set the Extrusion End value at-2'0". This *negative* value is measured *toward* the viewer from the work plane.
    c. Click on Apply.

11. Click the Big Green Checkmark (Finish Model) button to finish the model. See figure 16.4-B.

12. Go to the default 3-D view and check the positioning of the void form. See figure 16.4-C. The end of the roof should be entirely inside of the void form. Use the blue shape handles to adjust the start and end planes of the void form as needed to capture the entire end of the roof object, while extending a short distance outside of the roof's eaves on each side.

Next we use the void form we just created to cut off the end of the solid roof object. For this we use the Cut Geometry tool. See figure 16.4-D.

1. In Roof Plan view, go to Modify tab > Geometry panel > Cut button.
2. Hover over the edge lines of the roof object and verify that its outlines turn blue. Click on it to select the roof object.
3. Hover over the void extrusion form and verify that its outlines turn blue. Click on it. You should now see that the void extrusion vanishes and the roof has been cut.
4. Click the Finish Model (Big Green Checkmark) button in the ribbon to complete the cut of the roof. See figure 16.4-B.
5. The void form vanishes, and the roof is cut. Verify the correctness of the cut in both 3-D default view and in elevation.
6. Repeat the void extrusion procedure for the other end of the roof as needed.

If void extrusions are needed for both ends of a roof object, they can both be drawn in the same Sketch Mode operation to save time. You can use the Mirror tool to mirror the first void extrusion form to the other end of the gable roof. Be sure to cut both void forms from the roof object.

Editing the Void Extrusion Form

At times you may find that you need to select and edit the void extrusion after the roof has been cut. This procedure is a bit tricky, mainly because of the limited visual feedback provided by Revit. This is the procedure for selecting and editing the void extrusion form:

1. Go to the view where you can easily see the change you want to make. In this example, let's go to the Side Elevation view.

2. Hover over the slanted edge of the roof where the void extrusion was used to cut the roof. Notice that the edge line of the roof turns blue, and a tooltip appears with the words "Roofs: Void 01: Void 01." Click on the blue edge. Nothing changes on the screen. That's okay; just have faith.

3. In the ribbon, click on the Edit In-Place button. You are now taken to Sketch Mode. You can see the red X and the Big Green Checkmark button in the ribbon.

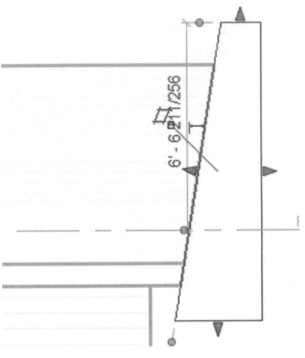

Figure 16.5. Editing the void extrusion

4. Hover over the slanted, cut edge of the roof again. Look very close— you can see four tiny purple points that define the corners of the void extrusion.

5. Click on the cut edge of the roof. Now the edges of the void extrusion are visible in blue, with shape handles available. See figure 16.5.

The void extrusion is now ready to be edited using the shape handles. If you need to redraw or change the lines of the sketch, click the Edit Extrusion button in the green Mode panel. When you're done with editing, click the Big Green Checkmark (Finish Model) button in the ribbon. Done!

This method of cutting away part of a roof object using an extruded void form is useful in many situations that you run across in modeling roofs in Revit. It's a great tool to have in your toolbox.

Chapter 17

Modeling the Half-Hip Roof

Figure 17.1. A traditional house with a half-hip roof

The half-hip roof appears to be a merging of a hip roof on top combined with a gable roof on the bottom. It also may be known by any of these colorful names:

- jerkinhead roof
- jerkin head roof
- half-hipped roof
- clipped gable
- jerkinhead gable
- hip-on-gable

The method Revit gives us to model this roof shape is very easy to use once you know it, but it is probably not what you would expect. Let's go through the steps.

95

Procedure for Creating a Half–Hip Roof

This example uses two overhang dimensions to form the roof's shape: 2'0" at the sides and 1'0" at the ends.

Prepare four supporting walls, with the tops of the walls justified to the level "First Floor Plate." The plan view dimensions of the building in this example are twenty feet by fifteen feet. Next we make the roof:

1. Click on the Roof by Footprint tool.
2. In the Properties box:
    a. Verify that the Roof Type you want is shown in the Selection Pane of the Properties dialog box.
    b. Set the Base Level in the Properties box to First Floor Plate.

3. In the Options bar:
    a. Verify that the Defines Slope option is checked.
    b. Verify that the Overhang distance is 2'0".
    c. Check the Extend to Wall Core option.

4. Using the Pick Walls tool, click on the north and south walls *only.*
5. Change the Overhang distance to 1'0" and click on the east and west walls.
6. In the Properties box, change the Rafter or Truss setting to Rafter.
7. If desired, change the Slope setting in the Properties box. I used the default 9" / 12" slope.
8. While still in Sketch Mode, click the Modify button in the ribbon.
9. Select the east and west edge lines. See figure 17.2-E. In the Properties box, change the Plate Offset from Base setting for these two edges to 3'6".

> Note: This 3'-6" dimension is entirely an aesthetic decision by the designer. It controls the vertical dimension from the plate height of the gable-shaped side roof edges up to the plate height of the half-hip roofs on the ends of the building. See figure 17.2-D. You can vary this dimension as needed for the proportions of your building.

10. Click the Big Green Checkmark in the Mode panel to accept the sketch.

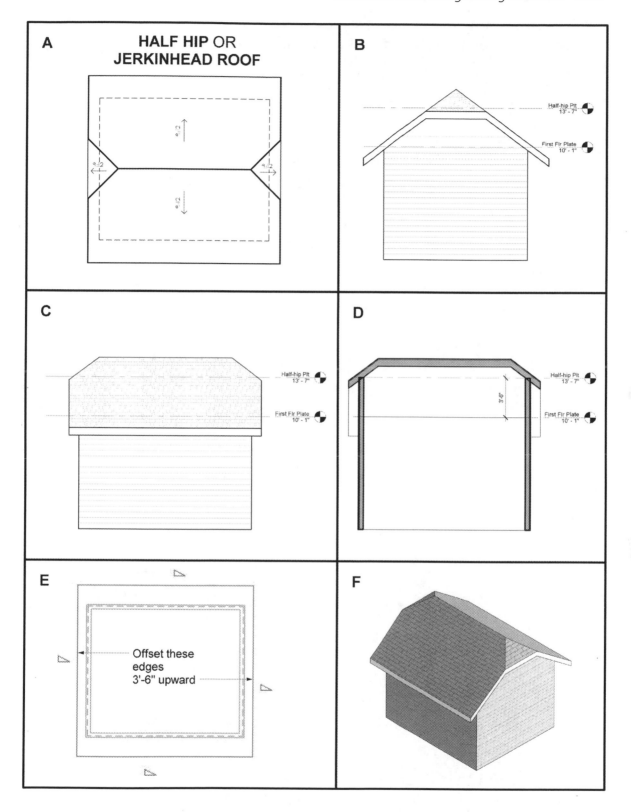

Figure 17.2. Six views of the half-hip roof

In the Default 3-D view, you will see that the roof is created properly, but the walls do not meet the roof on the east and west ends of the building. See figure 17.3-A. There are two ways to correct this:

1.   Quick and easy, by using the Attach Top/Base tool.
2.   If accurate section views are desired, use the Edit Profile tool.

First, here's the "quick and easy" method: Select the two end walls, click on the Attach Top/Base button, and click on the roof to close the gap between the walls and the roof. Done!

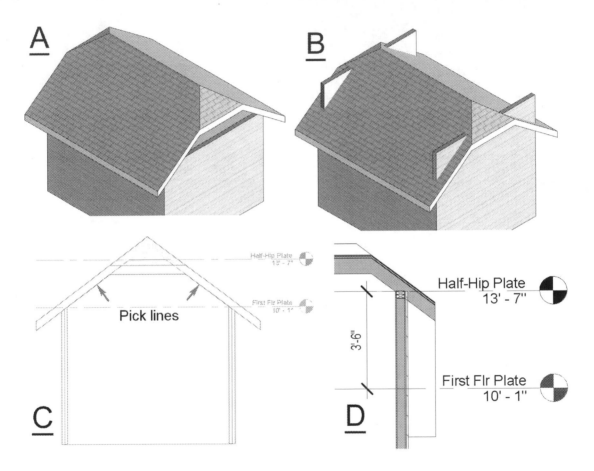

Figure 17.3. Adjusting the end walls of the half-hip building

Now we'll discuss the second method, which yields accurate Section views but takes more steps:

1.   Create a new Level datum and name it "Half-Hip Plate." Set the height at 3'6" above the First Floor Plate. See figure 17.3. This 3'6" dimension matches the Plate Offset from Base setting that we used in making the half-hip ends of the roof. (As discussed earlier, it's best to use the Copy tool to create the datum, not the button in the Datum panel of the ribbon. In this way, we avoid creating "junk" views.)

2. Select the east and west walls. Change the Top Constraint for these walls to Up to Level: Half-hip Plate. Your roof should now look like figure 17-3-B.

3. In the End Elevation view, select the end wall and click Edit Profile. (This is found in Modify | Walls tab > Mode panel.) You are taken to Sketch Mode.

4. Using the Pick Lines tool, click on the undersides of the raked fasciae. See figure 17.3-C.

5. Trim the lines as needed. Click the Big Green Checkmark to accept your sketch and change the wall's profile.

6. Your roof should now look similar to figure 17.2-F, and a Section view through the end wall should look like figure 17.3-D.

Done! This roof looks great in any view.

Dimensions of the Half-Hip Roof

Note that the Plate Offset from Base setting can be any dimension that the designer wants, as long as it's less than the plate-to-ridge height. The larger the offset dimension, the smaller the half-hip part of the roof.

Also note that the eave-to-eave vertical dimension

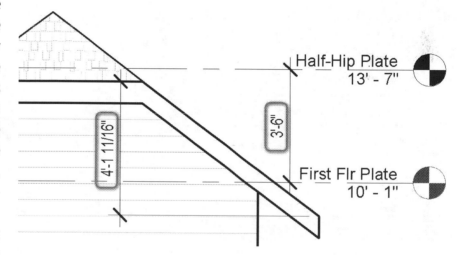

Figure 17.4. These two dimensions may not always match

(see figure 17.4) visible on the exterior of the building will not necessarily be equal to the Plate Offset from Base setting. The former dimension is affected by the length of the overhangs and by the slope ratios. If the overhangs and slopes are equal, these two dimensions will be equal. If not, they will vary.

I find it interesting that this roof shape can be created simply by offsetting the height of the two end walls upward. This is a powerful technique with many other uses in Revit.

Next we will look at a roof shape that is the opposite of the jerkinhead roof.

Chapter 18

Modeling the Dutch Hip Roof

Figure 18.1. A Dutch hip roof with an inset window

The Dutch hip roof is in a way the opposite of the half-hip roof. It puts the gable roof on top and merges it with a hip roof below.

It is sometimes called a gable-on-hip roof or a Dutch gable. The small gable on top is sometimes referred to as a *gablet*.

This roof shape needs to be modeled in two parts: the lower, hip-shaped roof object first, followed by the upper, gable-shaped roof object. In this way, you can create a hole in top of the lower hip roof and use the edges of the hole as the justification for the upper, gable-shaped roof.

We will use the Roof Cutoff settings to create a perfectly centered hole in the lower hip roof.

Procedure for Creating a Dutch Hip Roof

First the bottom roof, followed by the upper "gablet" roof.

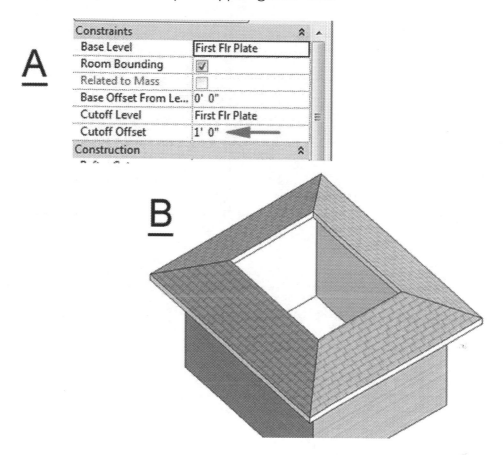

Figure 18.2. Hip roof with cutoff top

1. Create a hip roof as described in the hip roof procedure in chapter 13. Make the slope of the roof 6" / 12".
2. Select the hip roof object you just made and go to the Properties box. Under Constraints, click in the cell to the right of Cutoff Level. A pull-down arrow appears; click on it.
3. From the pull-down list, select First Floor Plate. Then set the Cutoff Offset in the Properties box to be 1'0". See figure 18.2-A.
4. The hip roof will now have a rectangular hole in its top. See figure 18.2-B.

Now we will create the upper, gable-shaped part of the roof.

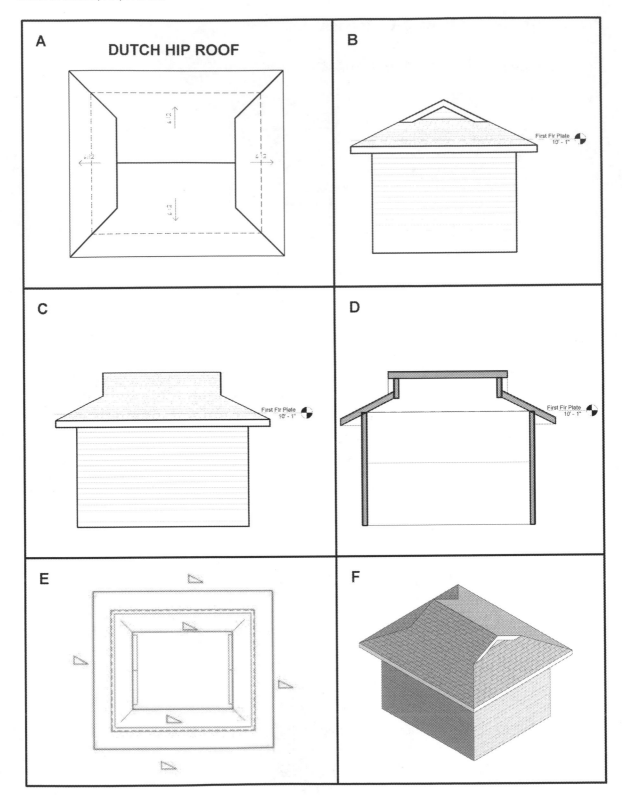

Figure 18.3. Six views of the Dutch hip roof

In Roof Plan view, ensure that the Work Plane is set to be First Floor Plate.

Then:

1. Click on the Roof by Footprint tool. In the Modify | Create Roof Footprint tab, in the Draw panel, click on the Pick Lines tool.
2. Click on the edges of the existing rectangular opening of the lower roof. The north and south edges will be slope originating, as indicated by the arrows in figure 18.4-A. Edit the slope ratios of these edges to match the slope of the lower roof.
3. Uncheck the Defines Slope option in the Options bar, and click on the east and west edges. These will become the gable ends. Again, these edges are *not* to be slope originating.
4. In the Properties box, set the Base Offset from Level value to be 1'0" (matching the Cutoff Offset value in figure 18.2-A above). Ensure that the Cutoff Level value is set to None. See figure 18.4-B. Click on Apply.
5. Click on the Big Green Checkmark in the Mode panel. You should have a gable roof sitting atop a hip roof as shown in figure 18.4-C.
6. Go to the Section view to verify alignment and adjust the heights as needed. Figure 18.5-A shows the perfect alignments at the critical connections (circled).
7. Once the roofs are aligned, use the Geometry > Join tool to join the upper and lower roots together. See figure 18.5-B.

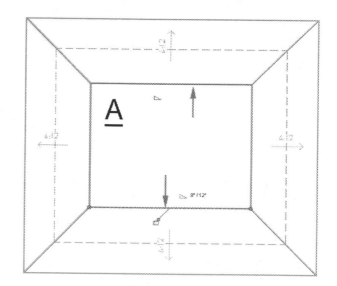

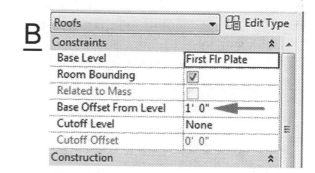

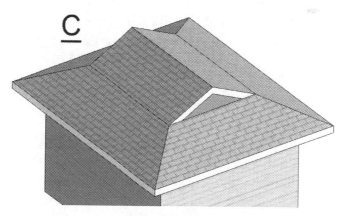

Figure 18.4. Making the top gablet roof

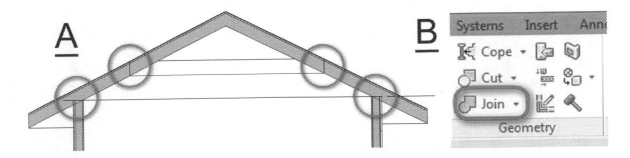

Figure 18.5. The critical alignment points in the Dutch hip roof

Adding Recessed Knee Walls to the Gable Ends

Knee walls need to be added within the triangular openings at the gable ends of the roof. Typically these walls are set back six inches or so behind the ends of the gable roof. See the Section view in figure 18.3-D. This is done as follows:

1. In Roof Plan view, set the work plane to be the First Floor Plate.
2. Create a wall extending from the north edge of the gable roof to the south edge. See figure 18.6-A. Set the wall back six inches from the roof's edge as shown.
3. Make the wall's Top Constraint "Unconnected," and set the height to 3'0".
4. Go to Default 3-D view and use the Attach Top/Base tool to attach the wall to the upper roof. See figure 18.5-B.

Now we need to modify the lower roof. We need to extend the east face of the lower roof upward an extra three inches vertically and six inches horizontally (assuming a 6" / 12" slope) to terminate at the triangular knee walls.

This can be done easily, using the Base Offset From Level setting.

1. Go to the Default 3-D view and select the lower roof object.
2. In the Properties box, change the Cutoff Offset setting from 1'0" to 1'3". See figure 18.6-B.

The roof should now extend up so that it terminates at the triangular knee wall, as shown in figure 18.6-C.

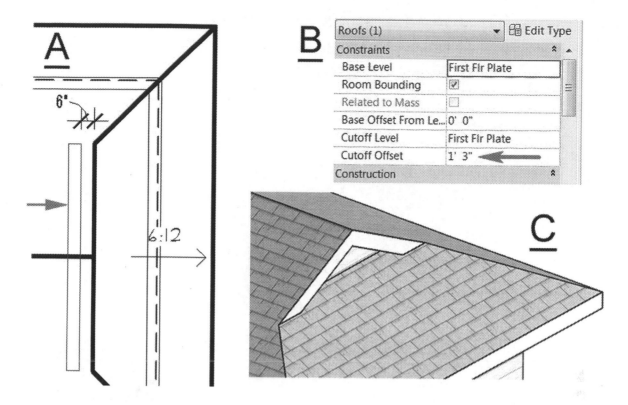

Figure 18.6. Making the triangular knee walls

We will now join the upper and lower roofs into one object. The purpose of joining the roofs together is to eliminate the unwanted line (or lines) where the roofs overlap or meet, both in plan, elevation, section, and 3-D views. The Join tool only works in eliminating the line(s) if the alignment between the two roofs is perfect.

For the Join tool to work correctly, the alignment between the two roofs must be perfect.

Select one roof, then go to Modify tab > Geometry panel > Join button. See figure 18.5-B. Click first on one roof, then on the other. Your building should look like figure 18.3-F, and you're done!

Group C: Complex Rectangular Roofs

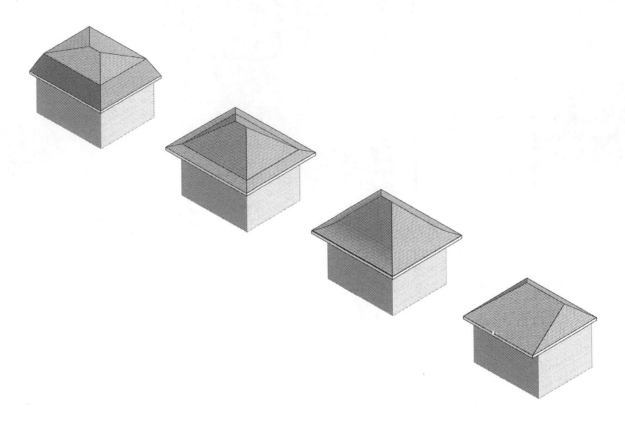

The Mansard Roof

The Two-Slope Roof

The Bell Roof

The Bastard Hip Roof

Chapter 19

Modeling the Mansard Roof

Figure 19.1. A beautifully detailed, traditional mansard roof house

The mansard roof consists of an upper hip roof constructed atop a bottom hip roof. The typical mansard roof has a very low-slope hip roof on top, making it invisible from the street, with a very visible, steeply sloped roof below.

The lower roof in the following exercise has straight sides. To model a bell-shape roof, as shown in the house in figure 19.1 above, refer to the procedure in chapter 21. The same methodology can be applied to the mansard roof.

Also referred to as a French roof or curb roof, this style of roof was popularized by the French architect Francois Mansart in the early seventeenth century. The lower roof is typically articulated by the addition of dormers and chimneys.

Procedure for Creating a Mansard Roof

The best procedure for creating a mansard roof involves using a *void form* to cut off the top of a very tall hip roof object. Here are the steps:

1. Prepare four supporting walls, with the top constraints of the walls set to "First Floor Plate." The Plan view dimensions of the building in this example are twenty feet by fifteen feet.
2. In Roof Plan view, set the work plane to Level: First Floor Plate (go to Architecture tab > Work Plane panel > Set). Click on the Roof by Footprint tool.
3. Verify that the Roof Type you want is shown in the Selection Pane of the Properties dialog box.
4. In the Options bar:
   a. Ensure that the Defines Slope option is checked.
   b. Set the desired Overhang distance to be 1'0".
   c. Check the Extend to wall core option.

5. Using the Pick Walls tool, click on the four walls, moving in a clockwise direction. You should now have four magenta lines, each with a slope triangle.
6. In the Properties box:
   a. Change the Slope setting (under Dimensions) to 24" / 12".
   b. Choose Rafter in the Rafter or Truss option.
   c. Click on the Apply button.

7. Check the sketch to ensure proper corner connections and slope definitions. Then click the Big Green Checkmark button to accept the sketch and create the 3-D roof.

Having created the lower roof, we now need to cut off its top, using a void form.

1. Go to the End Elevation view and draw a detail line 3'0" above the First Floor Plate level. This represents the future top of the lower roof object.
2. Go to Architecture tab > Build panel > Component flyout menu and click on the Model In-Place button. See figure 19.3-A.

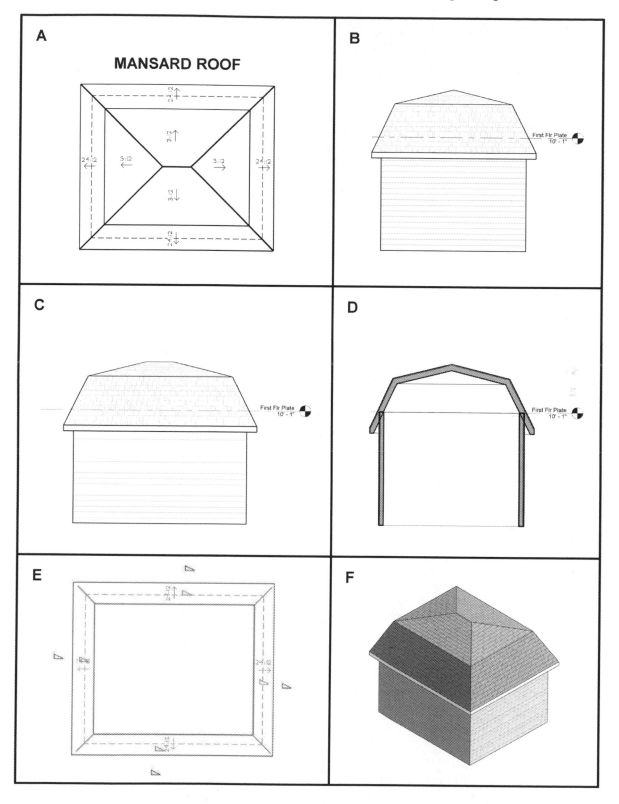

Figure 19.2. Six views of the mansard roof

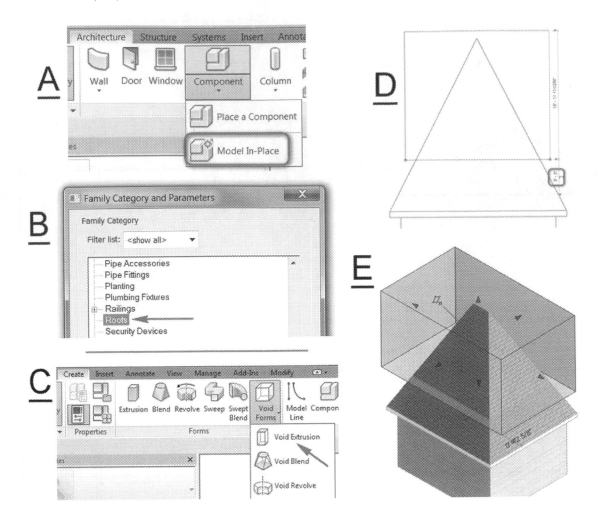

Figure 19.3. Making a void extrusion

3. In the Family Category and Parameters dialog box, choose Roofs. See figure 19.3-B. Click on OK.
4. In the Name dialog box, enter the name "Void 01." Click on OK.
5. Go to Create tab > Forms panel > Void Forms flyout menu and click on Void Extrusion. See figure 19.3-C.
6. In the Work Plane dialog box, verify that the radio button for Pick a plane is selected, and hit OK. Next you will pick the new work plane.
7. Hover over the end wall. A blue line will appear around three sides of the wall, and a tooltip box will appear saying "Walls: Basic wall etc." Click on the wall to set the work plane.
8. The active tab in the ribbon should say "Modify | Create Void Extrusion," and you are in Sketch Mode. Select the Rectangle tool in the green-colored Draw panel.
9. Using the Rectangle tool, draw a rectangle similar to that shown in figure 19.3-D.

10. In the Properties box:
    a. Set the Extrusion Start value at 18'0". This *positive* value is measured *away from* the viewer from the work plane.
    b. Set the Extrusion End value at-2'0". This *negative* value is measured *toward* the viewer from the work plane.

11. Click on Apply in the Properties box.

Click the Big Green Checkmark (Finish Edit Mode) button to accept the sketch. You should now see four shape handles. Go to the default 3-D view and check the positioning of the void form. See figure 19.3-E. The upper part of the roof should be entirely inside of the void form. Use the blue shape handles as needed to adjust the planes of the void form to capture the entire upper roof, while extending a short distance outside of the roof. Click on the Big Green Checkmark.

Next we will cut the void form we just created from the solid roof object. For this we use the Cut Geometry tool.

1. In Default 3-D view, click on Modify tab > Geometry panel > Cut button. The void form turns yellow-colored.
2. Hover over any edge line of the void extrusion and verify that its outlines turn blue. Click on it to select the void form.
3. Now hover over the roof object and verify that its outlines turn blue. Click on it. You should now see that the void extrusion vanishes, and the roof has been cut. See figure 19.4-A.
4. Click the Big Green Checkmark (Finish Model) button in the ribbon to complete the cutting of the roof.

Now we will create the upper hip roof as follows:

1. In Roof Plan view, click on the Roof by Footprint button. You are now in Sketch Mode.

2. Change the work plane to First Floor Plate by going Modify > Work Plane > Set button and selecting First Floor Plate from the list.

3. Select the Pick Lines tool in the Draw panel. Click on the four outside lines forming the top of the lower roof. See figure 19.4-B.

4. In the Properties box:

   a. Under Constraints, change the Base Offset from Level setting to 3'0". This matches the dimension that we used to make the top plane of the lower roof.

   b. Under Dimensions, change the Slope setting to 3" / 12".

   c. Hit the Apply button.

5. Click on the Big Green Checkmark to accept the sketch. You will find that the upper roof is sitting too high. See figure 19.4-C.

6. Go to the Section view to lower the position of the upper roof so that the two roofs are meeting properly. You will need to lower the upper roof (using the Move tool) so that the top edge of the upper roof aligns with the top edge of the lower roof.

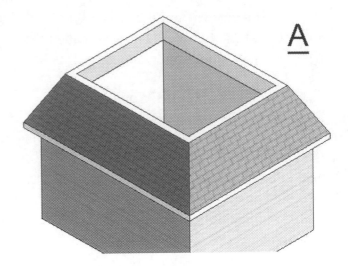

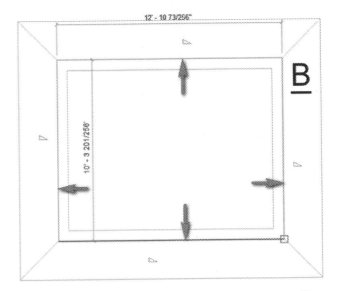

Figure 19.4. Modeling the upper roof

You can then use the Geometry > Join tool to join the two roofs together. This improves the appearance of the roof connection in Section views. See figure 19.2-D.

Done!

An Alternative Method

The method described above for creating a mansard roof takes quite a large number of steps. You can save some time by using the Cutoff Level and Cutoff Offset settings, instead of a void extrusion, to cut off the lower roof. However, the section view is not as realistic, since the Cutoff tool makes a vertical cut instead of the horizontal cut produced by the void extrusion. This is only a problem in section views.

If the section view is not important to you, then you can use the quicker Cutoff method, which is described in the next chapter, "Modeling the Two-Slope Roof."

Chapter 20

Modeling the Two-Slope Roof

Figure 20.1. A two-slope gable roof with dramatic, deep overhangs

The two-slope roof is actually an upper hip roof sitting atop a lower hip roof. The lower hip typically has a relatively low slope. It is sometimes called a *sprocket roof*.

The same two-slope arrangement can be applied to gable roofs as well, as shown in figure 20.1, but in the exercise below, we will assume a wraparound hip shape. The lower roof may be wide enough to cover a porch, or it may only consist of a narrow skirt, adding a flared shape to the bottom of the roof.

From a construction standpoint, it's helpful to have a supporting wall at the point where the lower roof joins the upper roof. In this way, the wall can be used to support both roofs. This arrangement also tends to work well from a visual standpoint.

Procedure for Creating a Two-Slope Roof

We will begin by creating the bottom "skirt" part of the roof.

1. Prepare four supporting walls, with the top constraints of the walls set to "First Floor Plate." The plan view dimensions of the building in this example are twenty feet by fifteen feet.
2. In Roof Plan view, set the work plane to Level: First Floor Plate (go to Architecture tab > Work Plane panel > Set).
3. Click on the Roof by Footprint tool.
4. Verify that the Roof Type you want is shown in the Selection Pane of the Properties dialog box.
5. In the Options bar:
   a. Ensure that the Defines Slope option is checked.
   b. Set the desired Overhang distance to be 2'0".
   c. Check the Extend to wall core option.

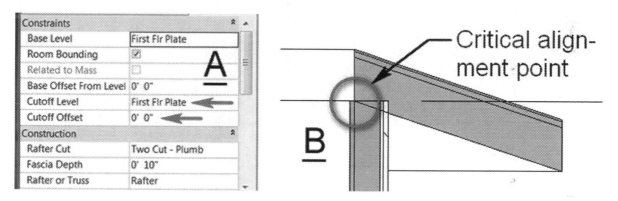

Figure 20.2. Creating the lower roof object

6. In the Properties box, set the Cutoff Level to First Floor Plate, and keep the default Cutoff Offset set to 0'0". See figure 20.2-A. Click on the Apply button. (Note that the Cutoff Offset setting measures the vertical distance from the selected cutoff level to the bottom edge of the roof rafter zone at the Cutoff Level, not the top edge. In this case, that distance is zero.)
7. Using the Pick Walls tool, click on the four walls, moving in a clockwise direction. You should now have four magenta lines, each with a slope triangle.

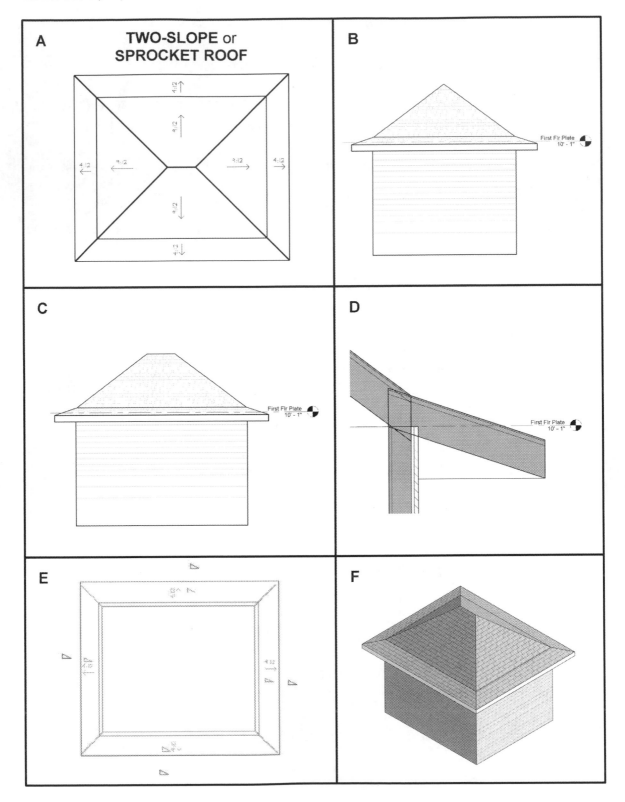

Figure 20.3. Six views of the two-slope or sprocket roof

8. In the Properties box:
    a. Change the Slope setting (under Dimensions) to 4" / 12". (This is much faster than changing the slope settings of all the edges.)
    b. Choose Rafter in the Rafter or Truss option. Click on the Apply button.

9. Check the sketch to ensure proper corner connections and slope definitions, then click the Big Green Checkmark button in the ribbon to accept the sketch and create the 3-D roof. Your section view should look like figure 20.2-B.

Now we will create the upper hip roof as follows:

1. In Roof Plan view, click on the Roof by Footprint button. You are again in Sketch Mode.
2. In the Options bar:
    a. Ensure that the Defines Slope option is checked.
    b. Set the desired Overhang distance to be 0'0".

3. Check the Extend to wall core option.
4. In the Properties box, set the Cutoff Level to None, and keep the default Cutoff Offset set to 0'0". Click on the Apply button.
5. Using the Pick Walls tool, click on the four walls, moving in a clockwise direction. You should now have four magenta lines, each with a slope triangle.
6. In the Properties box:
    a. Change the Slope setting (under Dimensions) to 9" / 12".
    b. Choose Rafter in the Rafter or Truss option. Click on the Apply button.

7. Check the sketch to ensure proper corner connections and slope definitions, then click the Big Green Checkmark button in the ribbon to accept the sketch and create the 3-D roof.
8. Go to the Section view and verify that the upper and lower roofs are meeting properly. See figure 20.3-D. The rafters will actually overlap like this in real-world built form.

Done!

Chapter 21

Modeling the Bell Roof

Figure 21.1. Graceful bell-shaped eaves on a tile-roofed house

The bell roof is similar to the two-slope roof, with a special added element smoothing the connection between the upper and lower roofs. I call this element the *swoop*. It's a curving, arc-shaped roof surface connecting and blending the upper roof to the lower roof. Typically, the upper roof has a steeper slope and the lower roof has a gentler slope.

This overall roof shape is sometimes known as a bell-cast eave roof, or a bell-cast roof, referring to the cross-section shape of a bell.

It's visually important that the swoop meets the upper and lower roofs in a tangential manner. There should be a perfectly smooth blending between the curving swoop and the slopes of the top and bottom roofs, with no visible bump or joint where they meet. By following the method described below, you will end up with a graceful, bump-free, bell-shaped roof.

The radius of the swoop is up to the preference of the designer. The following procedure uses a radius that is equal to the roof's overhang. In this way, the swoop is as large as possible, given the size of the overhang.

Procedure for Creating a Bell Roof

Begin by carrying out all the steps in the two-slope roof procedure in chapter 20. For this exercise, make the slope of the upper roof 12" / 12" and the slope of the lower roof 4" / 12". See figure 21.3-A.

Here's how we make the arc for the roof extrusion:

1. In the Section view, zoom in on the point where the top surfaces of the upper and lower roofs come together. Mark this point with a circle (using a detail line). See figure 21.3-A.
2. Referring to figure 21.3-B, draw an arc (using a detail line) with its center point at the intersection of the two roofs. Make the arc radius 2'0", the dimension that matches our 2'0" overhang. At each of the points where the arc ends on the surfaces of the upper and lower roofs, I've drawn a circle.
3. Next we go to the lower roof. Referring to figure 21.3-C, draw a line of any length, perpendicular to the lower roof and ending at the roof surface. Move that line so that its endpoint lies on the lower endpoint of the arc.
4. Go to the upper roof and repeat the above step. Draw a line of any length, perpendicular to the upper roof and ending at the roof surface. Move that line so that its endpoint lies on the upper endpoint of the arc.
5. Draw a third detail line from the two roofs' intersection point to the midpoint of the arc.
6. Extend the three detail lines from steps 3, 4, and 5 to a point where they (ideally) all intersect perfectly. Mark this point with a circle. See figure 21.3-C. This will become the center point for the extruded swoop of the roof.
7. Using the same procedure that we used in chapter 14 to create the barrel roof, create an arc-shaped roof by extrusion as shown in figure 21.3-D. Use the intersection from step 6 as the arc's center point. Click on the Big Green Checkmark to accept the sketch.

The next step is to trim the extruded roof object. In the Default 3-D view, the roof should look something like figure 21.4. The extruded swoop may extend beyond the roof on both ends. That's okay. The next step is to trim it to size, using vertical openings.

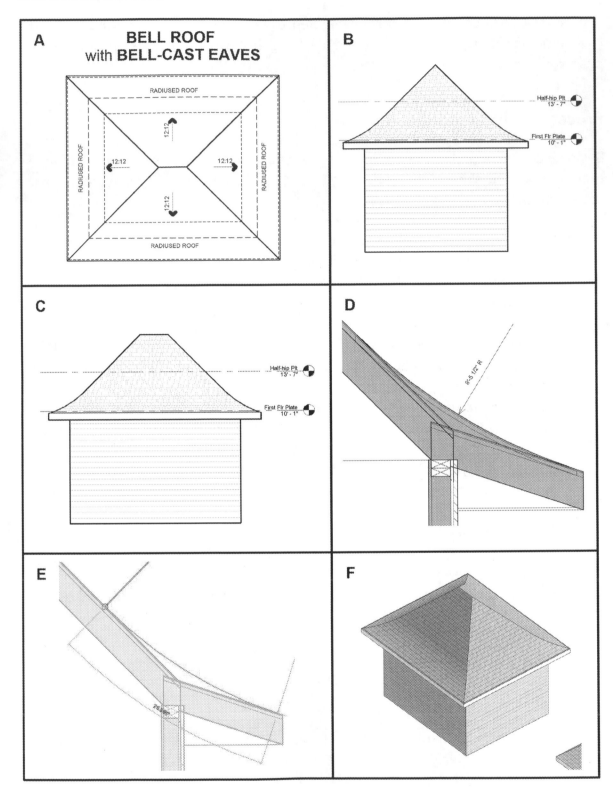

Figure 21.2. Six views of the bell roof

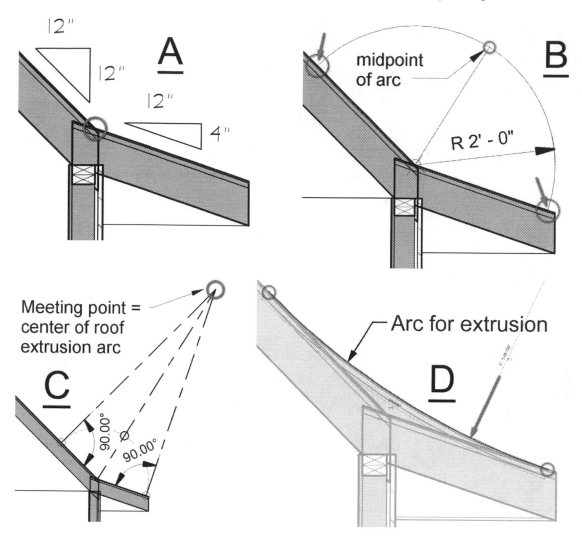

Figure 21.3. Creating the swoop of the bell roof

In Roof Plan or the Default 3-D view, adjust the length of the extrusion (using the shape handles) so that extrusion's ends extend a few feet beyond the east and west edges of the roof. See figure 21.4-A.

1. Now we will use the Vertical Opening tool to trim the ends of the swoop extrusion to a forty-five-degree angle. Select the extruded roof object. In the Opening panel of the ribbon, click on Vertical Opening button. You are taken to Sketch Mode.
2. Draw a sketch containing two line loops, similar to the loops shown figure 21.4-A. The forty-five-degree lines should be perfectly aligned with the hip lines of the roof. Be sure that the loop of lines completely encloses the end of the extrusion.
3. Click on the Big Green Checkmark to accept your sketch and trim the swoop.

You now have a bell roof on one side of your building. Let's work on the second side.

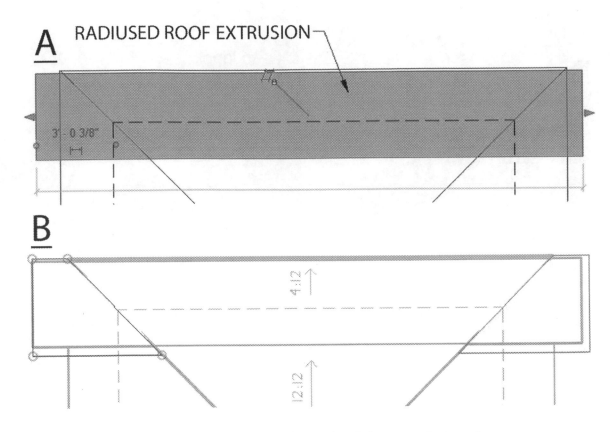

Figure 21.4. Trimming the ends of the extruded roof

Using the Mirror – Pick Axis tool, mirror the trimmed extrusion object to the right (east) side of the building, using the hip line for the mirror axis. Trim this extrusion to the hip lines as follows:

1. Activate the vertical opening by hovering over the (invisible) vertical opening and watch for a blue line to appear along the trimmed edge. When you see it, click with your mouse.
2. Click on Edit Extrusion in the ribbon. You should now see the outline of the vertical opening.
3. Modify the outline as needed, aligning the forty-five-degree line with the hip of the roof.
4. Click on the Big Green Checkmark to finalize your work.

Mirror the east extrusion (the one you just made) to the opposite (west) end of the roof. Also mirror the north extrusion to the south side of the roof. The roof should now look like the roof in figure 21.2-F. It took a lot of steps, but the result is worth it!

Breaking Free of the Work Plane

There is an issue that can arise when using the roof by extrusion method. When the roof needs to be moved or copied for whatever reason, it may refuse to be moved in any direction except one. This is caused by the extrusion being associated with a work plane. The solution to this problem is to break the extrusion free from its work plane. With the extruded roof object is selected, click on Edit Work Plane in the Work Plane panel of the ribbon. In the Work Plane dialog box, click on Dissociate. I've found this prevents issues later if the roof needs editing.

Sometimes the Dissociate button is grayed out. In these cases, I try to use the Mirror tool in place of the Copy, Move, or Rotate tools.

I'm free!

In the next chapter, we will discuss one of the most challenging roof types to model in Revit: the bastard hip. If the name is offensive to some ears, I apologize—there's really no other name for it.

Chapter 22

The Aptly Named Bastard Hip Roof

It's a Tricky One, That Bastard Hip Roof

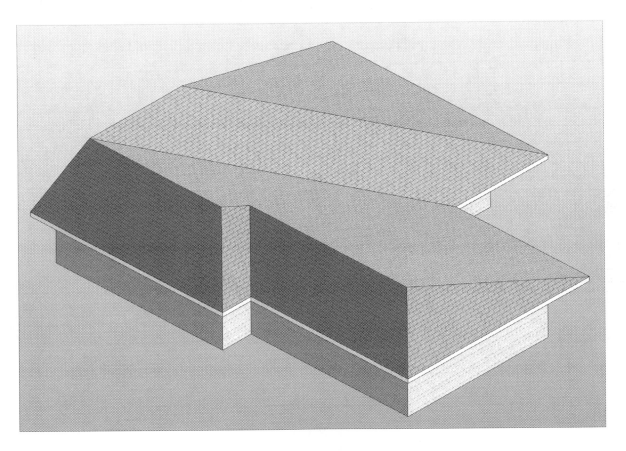

Figure 22.1. Revit model of a house on a corner lot with bastard hips

Bastard hips are very common in residential construction. You may have seen several examples of them and mistaken them for standard hip roofs. Bastard hip roofs and standard hip roofs look very similar from a ground-level view.

A bastard hip roof is a roof that has nonmatching slopes meeting at one or more hip lines. In other words, a steeper-sloped face and a shallower-sloped face meet, forming what is known as a bastard hip line.

The modeling of this roof in Revit is similar to modeling the hip roof, except that at least one of the roof faces has a different slope from at least one adjacent face. Viewed in Roof

Plan view, the bastard hip line has an angle that is not the typical forty-five-degree-angled line of a standard hip.

The house shown in figure 22.1 is designed to go on a corner lot. The street-facing, steeper roof faces have 24" / 12" slopes. The roof faces sloping toward the rear have gentler 4" / 12" slopes.

Why go to the trouble of using this type of roof? The bastard hip roof is often used to present a steeper, more traditional-looking roof profile to the public sides of the house while covering large areas of floor area with a more economical, gentler slope in the rear. Another reason is to make ridge lines align where they would not align using standard hip roofs.

This type of roof can be a bit challenging in Revit if you are, like me, really particular about alignments and clean connections at the detail level of design. It is doable; you just have to be ready to go through quite a number of steps to get the details perfect.

First, it will be helpful to review some roof terminology. Please refer back to figure 1.2 in chapter 1. The word "eave" is defined by *Merriam-Webster* as: "the lower border of a roof that overhangs the wall."

In other words, the eave is the *lower edge of a roof face,* typically a face that overhangs beyond a wall. Contrary to common usage, an eave is not the overhang; it is not the fascia; and it is not the soffit. It is the line formed at the bottom edge of the roof face, at an overhanging roof.

The word "fascia" is defined in *Merriam-Webster* as:

> a flat usually horizontal member of a building having the form of a flat band: as a horizontal piece (as a board) covering the joint between the top of a wall and the projecting eaves—called also fascia board.

In this chapter, we will use the word "fascia" to describe the planar surface naturally formed at the termination of the roof assembly, or "sandwich." This is subtly different from the additional trim object that you can apply to the roof using Revit's Roof Fascia tool.

The "fascia depth" is the distance from the eave (the lowest edge of the roof face) to the lowest part of the rafter zone, measured vertically.

Solving a Common Issue

When using the Roof by Footprint tool to create a bastard hip roof, Revit often tells you that it "Can't make footprint roof." When this happens, go to the Properties box and check the Rafter Cut and Fascia Depth settings.

If the Rafter Cut is set to Two Cut – Plumb or Two Cut - Square, and the Fascia Depth setting you're using is a small dimension such as 4", Revit will give you the above error message and refuse to create the roof object.

The solution is to increase the Fascia Depth setting to a dimension several inches larger than the overall thickness of the roof type assembly, or "sandwich." Revit will then be able to create the roof object. You can go back later and carefully decrease the Fascia Depth setting to achieve the two-cut shape you want, within Revit's limits.

For the examples in this chapter, I modeled the roof with a 2'0" overhang on all four sides, justified to the walls by using the Pick Walls tool. The north, east, and west faces have a 9" / 12" slope. The south face has a gentler 3" / 12" slope. Two of the resulting hips are normal, measuring forty-five degrees from the line of the roof's edge in Roof Plan view. The other two hip lines are bastard hips, which happen to fall at an angle of 18.43 degrees from the roof's east and west edge lines in the Roof Plan.

One of the quirks of bastard hips (in Revit and in actual construction) is that the hip line formed on *top* of the roof assembly does not align perfectly with the hip line formed on the underside of the assembly when viewed in Roof Plan view (see figure 22.2-A). Revit creates the bastard hip roof with all four underside hip lines crossing exactly over the points where the interior edges of the wall plates meet in Roof Plan view. These points are circled in figure 22.2-A.

When you first model this unequal-slope hip roof in Revit, using the Pick Walls tool and a 2'0" overhang, the eaves are created with weird, uneven heights, as shown in figure 22.2-B.

A section through this roof is shown in figure 22.2-C.

This strange roof shape is Revit's way of making all the rafter zones sit perfectly on the wall plates.

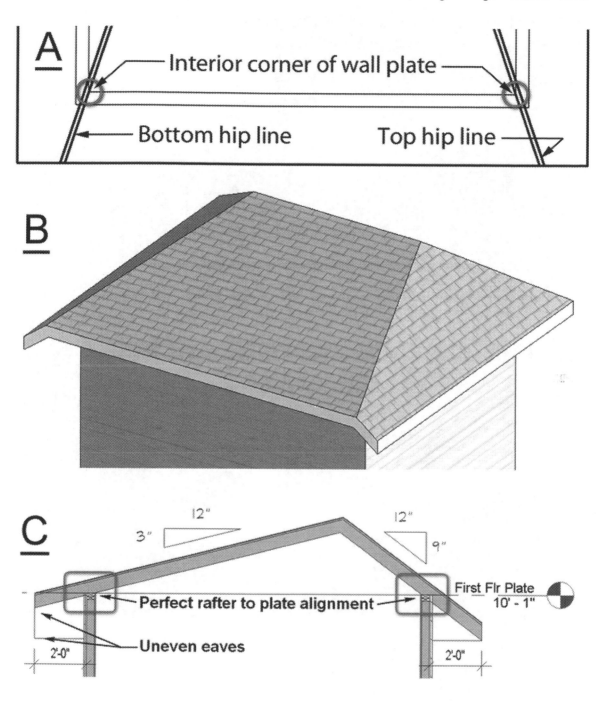

Figure 22.2. Unequal-slope hip roof before aligning eaves

This makes perfect sense from a construction standpoint. However, this is probably not the roof shape that you want to see from the exterior. As a designer, you would probably prefer that the eaves continue at the same height all around the building.

Fortunately, Revit gives you a special tool to align the eaves of your roof. It is called ... ready? ... "Align Eaves." It is available only in Sketch Mode, while you are creating or editing the roof's footprint. To find it, select the roof object, then click on Modify | Roofs tab > Mode panel > Edit Footprint button; then click on the Tools panel > Align Eaves button. That will unhide the buttons for two very important options:

- Adjust Height
- Adjust Overhang

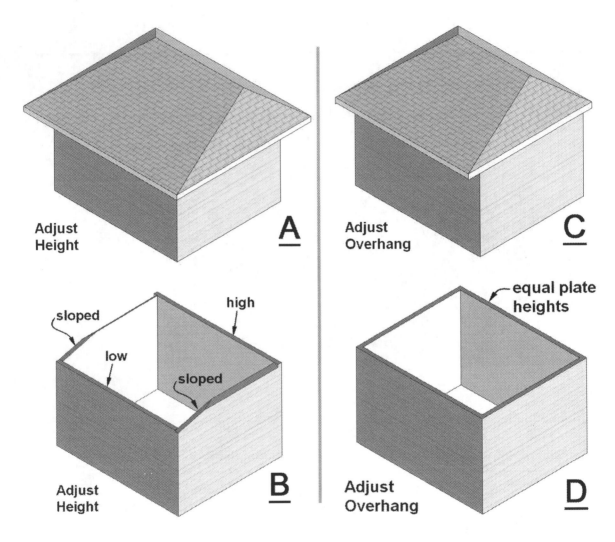

Figure 22.3. Two options for aligning eaves, shown with and without the roofs

These buttons represent two "flavors" of roof shape that the designer must choose between. They produce noticeably different shapes of roof, shown in figure 22.3. The best choice for your project depends upon your design preferences. The main aesthetic question is: are you willing to let Revit change the overhang dimensions of the various eaves, making some overhangs deeper and some shorter? If so, you will probably want to use the Adjust Overhang option. If, on the other hand, you want all overhangs to be equal, you will lean toward the Adjust Height option.

Let's look briefly at the two options and how they work:

- **Adjust Height.** See figures 22.3-A and B. This option keeps all the overhang dimensions as they were originally set and raises or lowers one or more eaves (as selected by the designer) to make them all align.
- **Adjust Overhang.** See figures 22.3-C and D. This option shortens or lengthens one or more of the overhangs (as selected by the designer) to make the eaves align while keeping the walls' top plate heights unchanged (meeting the rafters as they would in a standard hip roof).

Figure 22.3 shows the roof shape resulting from each option, as well as the wall shapes required to support the roofs properly.

Let's now discuss the two options in more depth.

"Adjust Height" Option Concepts

It helps to understand that the name of the "Adjust Height" option does not mean that it changes the height of the eave above the floor level—both of the options do that. The name stresses that it adjusts the eave height *only*—without changing the lengths of the overhangs. I think of it as grabbing the fascia that is causing the problem—in this case, the middle part of the south fascia (see figure 22.2-B)—and tugging it straight downward until it aligns with the others.

Several things happen when Revit makes this change:

- The bastard hip rafters cross over the wall plates a few feet away from the corners of the building—not at the building wall corners, as in a standard hip roof.
- The bastard hip rafter lines intersect the corners of the roof footprint perfectly in Plan view.
- The ridge line of the roof moves a small distance to the north.
- The plate heights of the east, west, and south walls now need to adjust to accommodate the new rafter arrangement. The Revit designer can easily make this change by using the Attach Top/Base tool to attach the walls to the modified roof.

The "Adjust Height" option roof shown in figure 22.3-A has an appearance that is pleasing and balanced, with equal overhangs all around. However, in figure 22.3-B, with the roof hidden, notice the varying wall heights required to support this roof shape. The north wall plate is at a higher level, the south plate is at a lower level, and the east and west wall plates are high along part of their length. Then they slope down in the areas near the intersections with the south wall.

This is easy for the Revit modeler, using the Attach Top/Base tool. We just make the roof first and then tell the walls to go up to the roof. However, it's not so easy for the builder, who cannot build the roof before building the walls.

> This discussion assumes the use of traditional rafter construction. If you are using truss construction methods, you can get the clean roof shape shown in figure 22.3-A, combined with the equal wall plate heights of figure 22.3-D.

The real-world builder must calculate the angles in the roof and build the complex, varying-height supporting walls before starting on the roof. Doable but not easy.

"Adjust Overhang" Option Concepts

With the Adjust Overhang option, you can either:

- Make the north, east, and west overhangs shorter, keeping the south overhang at the original dimension of two feet; or
- Make the south overhang longer, keeping the other three overhangs unchanged at two feet.

To understand what the Adjust Overhang option does in the first option, visualize the fasciae of the north, east, and west roof edges being dragged upward and inward at an angle exactly matching the slope of the roof, until they align with the fascia of the south (unchanged) eave.

The Adjust Overhang roof example shown in figure 22.3-C has a standard two-foot overhang for the south (lower slope) edge. After adjustment using the Align Eaves > Adjust Overhang tool, keeping the south overhang unchanged, the other three edges have an overhang of only 7 9/16"—much shorter than standard. While easier to build, the visual effect may not be ideal. The upside is that the supporting wall plate heights remain consistent for all walls, as shown in figure 22.3-D.

What if you want to keep 2'0" as the *minimum* overhang dimension and make the south edge's overhang longer? In that case, using the Adjust Overhang option, we find that the overhang of the south facing roof increases to 6'0"". This is obviously quite a large increase. See figure 22.4.

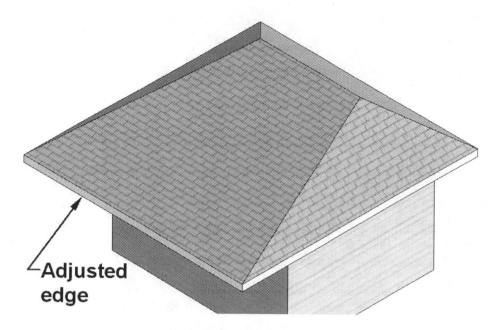

Adjusted edge

Figure 22.4. Making a very long (6'-0") overhang on the south edge is one way to align the eaves

Which of these is the better choice? It's up to the designer to weigh the pros and cons. Considering construction costs, Adjust Height is generally the more expensive option, and the Adjust Overhang option becomes the more affordable option. Will anyone really notice if the overhangs are different? That's the designer's call.

In order to clearly show how both of these Eave Aligning options work, we will now go through two roof-modeling exercises in this order:

Method 1: using Align Eaves > Adjust Height option, then

Method 2: using the Align Eaves > Adjust Overhang option.

Method 1: Making a Bastard Hip Roof Using the "Adjust Height" Option

1. Prepare four supporting walls, with the top constraints of the walls set to "First Floor Plate." The plan view dimensions of the building in this example are twenty feet by fifteen feet.
2. In Roof Plan view, set the work plane to Level: First Floor Plate.
3. Click on the Roof by Footprint tool.
4. Verify that the Roof Type you want is shown in the Selection Pane of the Properties dialog box.

5. In the Options bar:
   a. Ensure that the Defines Slope option is checked.
   b. Set the Overhang dimension to 2'0".
   c. Check the Extend to wall core option.

6. Using the Pick Walls tool, click on all four walls, moving in a clockwise direction, making sure that the overhang preview line is outside of the building. Hit the Escape key twice to exit the Pick Walls tool.

7. Select the south edge line and edit its slope ratio to be 3" / 12". Click outside of the editor box to save the change.

8. In the Properties box:
   a. Verify that the Base Level is set to First Floor Plate.
   b. Ensure that the Cutoff Level is set to None.
   c. Verify that the Rafter Cut option is set to Two Cut – Plumb.
   d. Verify that the Fascia Depth dimension is set to 1'0". This large number is intentional and important. A small number such as 4" may lead to error messages and failed attempts to create the bastard hip roof. You may be able to go back and reduce the fascia depth after the roof object has been created.
   e. In the Rafter or Truss setting in the Properties box, choose Rafter.
   f. Hit the Apply button.

9. Click the Big Green Checkmark button in the ribbon to accept the sketch and create the 3-D roof.

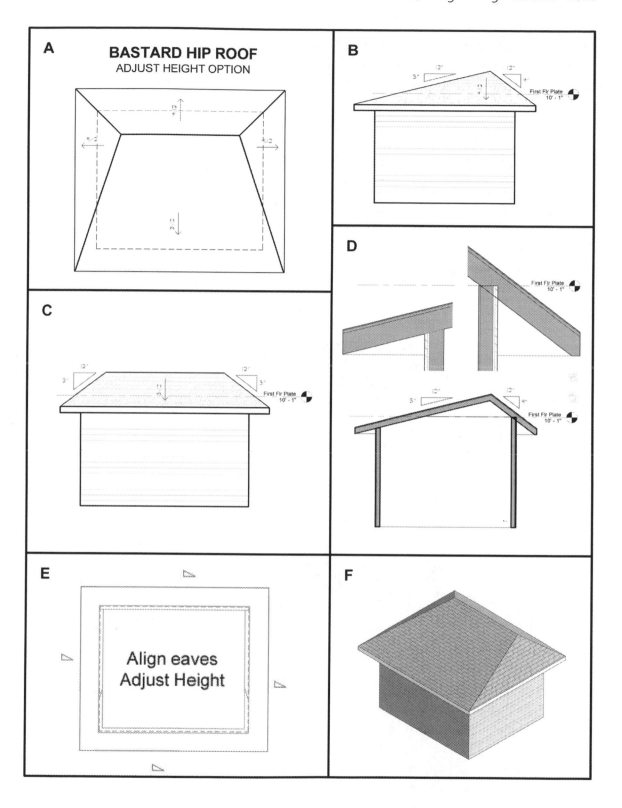

Figure 22.5. Six views of the bastard hip roof using the Adjust Height option

In the Default 3-D view, you will see that the eaves of the roof are not aligned. The south fascia has a strange up-over-and-down shape, as shown in figure 22.2-B.

Here is where we make use of the Align Eaves tool. For this first exercise, we will choose the Adjust Height option. Return to the Roof Plan view and:

1. Select the roof object and click on the Edit Footprint button. You're in Sketch Mode.
2. Click on the Align Eaves tool in the Tools panel.
3. Click on the Adjust Height button in the same panel.
4. Click first on the east (right) edge line of the roof and then on the south (bottom) edge line. No visual change is seen in Plan view. That's okay. We simply took the height above floor level of the east eave (the first edge clicked) and applied it to change the height of the south eave (the second edge clicked).
5. Click the Big Green Checkmark to accept the sketch and create the 3-D roof.

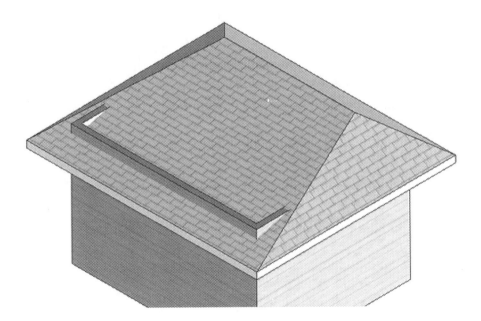

Figure 22.6. Nice roof, but obviously we have some wall height issues

In the Default 3-D view, we see that all the eaves and fasciae are now aligned and look perfect, as shown in figure 22.5. However, you can also see that parts of three walls are now poking through the roof, as shown in figure 22.6. This is a normal part of using the Adjust Height option tool and is easy to correct using the Attach Top/Base tool.

1. In 3-D view, select the east, south, and west walls, holding down the Ctrl key to select multiple objects.
2. Click on the Attach Top/Base tool in the Modify Wall panel of the ribbon.
3. Click on the linework of the roof object.

The walls are now trimmed and attached to the underside of the roof.

Your building should now appear similar to figure 22.5-F. The Section view should look like figure 22.5-D.

This completes the first half of the exercise, modeling the bastard hip using Method 1—Adjust Height. Next we will do the same building using Method 2—Adjust Overhang.

Method 2: Modeling a Bastard Hip Roof Using the "Adjust Overhang" Option

1. Follow (or repeat) steps 1 through 9 of the procedure shown in Method 1 (Adjust Height) above. You should now have a roof with varying slopes and varying eave heights, as shown in figure 22.2-B.
2. In the Roof Plan view, select the roof object and click on the Edit Footprint button. You are taken to Sketch Mode.
3. Click on the Align Eaves tool in the Tools panel of the ribbon.
4. This time, click on the Adjust Overhang button. This is where things start looking different.
5. First click on the south edge of the roof, indicated with arrow number 1 in figure 22.7-E. Then click on each of the other three edges (west, north, and east), numbered 2, 3, and 4 in the illustration. You will see their overhang dimensions decrease significantly.

Check the sketch to ensure proper corner connections and slope definitions. Then click the Big Green Checkmark button to accept the sketch and create the 3-D roof.

Go to the 3-D view. You will see that the top and bottom edges of the fasciae align perfectly. The roof will look similar to the one in figure 22.8.

However, if you intend to show section views, there is an issue of slight inaccuracies in the way that the rafters are not meeting the plates properly in all cases. This can be ignored, but it will affect the overhang dimensions. We will address that issue next.

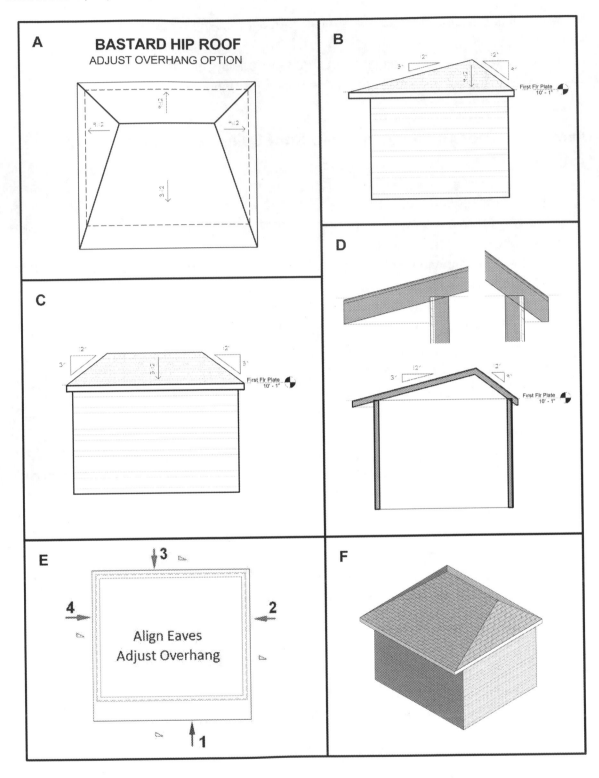

Figure 22.7. Six views of the bastard hip roof using the Adjust Overhang option

Correcting Rafter-Plate Alignments

Studying the roof in Section view, the rafters and studs do not join correctly on the north, east, and west eaves. Only the south eave looks correct. See figure 22.8.

This seems to be a flaw in the Align Eaves > Adjust Overhang tool. Here is the workaround that I use:

1. Open the Section view showing the north and south eaves. Zoom in on the south eave. Verify that the bottom edge of the rafter meets the top interior face of the stud perfectly at the First Floor Plate level line, as shown by a circle in figure 22.8-A.

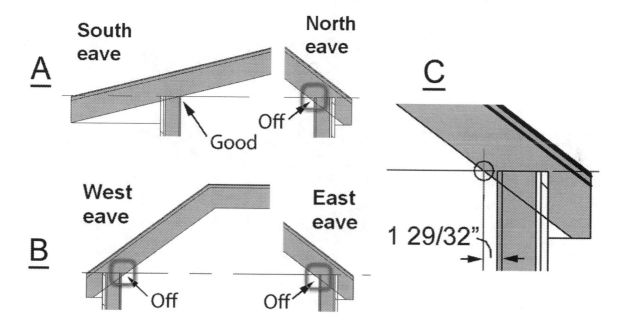

Figure 22.8. Misalignment issues

2. Now zoom in where the plate level line crosses the rafter at the north eave. The intersection is marked with a circle in figure 22.8-C. Draw a vertical detail line through this point, as shown.
3. Draw a high-precision dimension annotation between the vertical line created in step 2 and the interior face of the nearby stud wall. In this example, the dimension is 1 29/32" (see figure 22.9-C). This is the magic number that we will use to offset (move) the north, east, and south edge lines of the roof outward. This is our way of making the rafters meet the plates properly.

Return to Roof Plan view and select the roof object.

1. Click on the Edit Footprint tool in the ribbon.
2. Start the Offset tool. Its hot key is OF. In the ribbon, it's found in the Modify panel.

3. In the Options bar, set the Offset distance at 1 29/32", using the magic number from step 3 above.
4. Verify that the Copy option is unchecked. You want to move the lines, not copy.
5. Offset (move) the north, east, and west lines outward, away from the building.
6. Click on the Big Green Checkmark button to accept your sketch.

Check the rafter-to-roof alignments in the Section views through all four walls. They look good.

Aligning the Fasciae Bottom Edges

However, in 3-D view, I now find that the fasciae's bottom edges are not aligning properly at the southeast and southwest corners, as shown in figure 22.9-A.

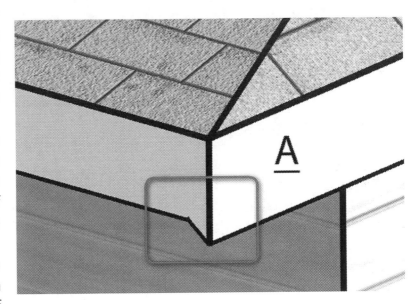

The best solution to this issue, in my opinion, is to decrease the Fascia Depth setting of the overall roof to match the depth of the south fascia.

Or if you're lazy, you can just apply a wide fascia board to all four sides of the roof, thereby hiding the problem, and call it a day.

If I try to simply change the Fascia Depth setting of the roof to a small measurement, say for example, 4", using the Properties dialog, Revit gives me an error message: "Can't make footprint roof." Apparently this error message only occurs in

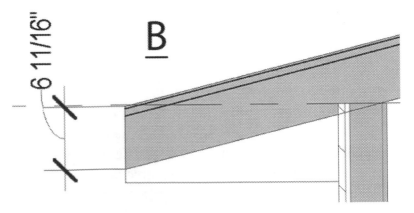

Figure 22.9. Misalignment at bottom edge of fascia

bastard hip roofs that were made using the Align Eaves > Adjust Overhang option. In regular hip roofs, or bastard hip roofs made using the Adjust Height option, Revit has no problem changing the fascia depth to a small number such as 4" or 5".

Time for another workaround. I've found that if I measure the depth of the narrowest fascia, add 1/16" to it, and use that sum for the Fascia Depth setting of the entire roof, Revit will accept that dimension, create the roof, and not give me an error message. That's my strategy.

The current depth of the narrowest fascia—the south fascia in this example—shows a dimension of 6 11/16". See figure 22.9-B. Adding 1/16" to that, to avoid dealing with Revit's error messages, we get 6 3/4". That is our magic number.

Select the roof, go to the Properties box, and change the Fascia Depth setting of the entire roof to 6 3/4". Success! The model is created.

Whew! After many steps, we finally have created a rectangular bastard hip roof with consistent wall plate heights all around, aligned eaves of equal height, adjusted overhangs, and perfect rafter-to-wall plate alignments on all sides. See figure 22.7-D.

Happy dance! (*Music plays*)

In summary, here's what we've learned:

1. Bastard hips are challenging in Revit and should be avoided altogether unless there's a compelling reason to use them.
2. To end up with a constant eave height, we use the Align Eaves tool, which requires us to choose between two flavors: Adjust Height and Adjust Overhang.
3. The Adjust Height option is quicker and easier to use, and it keeps all overhangs equal, but it makes the building more complex and expensive to build.
4. The Adjust Overhang option gives you a more buildable roof, but you get unequal overhangs and must deal with many detailing and alignment issues.

In short, bastard roofs are tricky in Revit. Come prepared with time and patience.

Group D: Circular and Polygonal Roofs

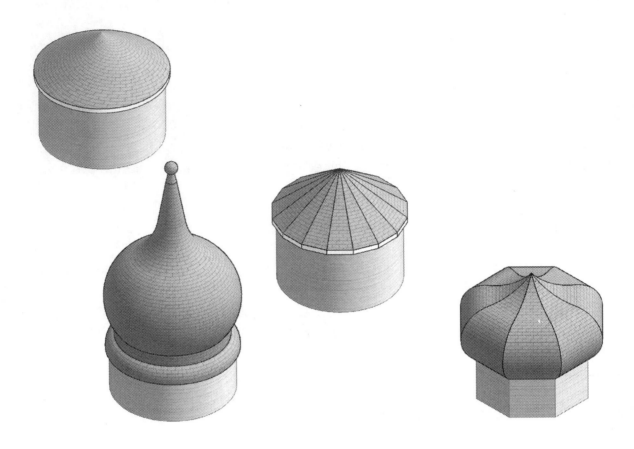

The Conical Roof

The Segmented Conical Roof

The Onion Dome Roof   •   The Segmented Dome Roof

Chapter 23

Modeling the Conical Roof

Figure 23.1. A half-circle conical roof joined to a gable roof

A conical roof conjures up images of turrets on castles, French chateaux, and damsels with unbelievably long hair. The shape makes a graceful counterpoint to the typical straight-edged roofs of most houses.

The conical roof is very easy to model in Revit. It's similar to the shed roof, except that the slope-defining edge is curved, not straight.

This can be used for a half-cone shape as well, as shown in the photo above; you simply draw a 180-degree arc for the footprint. A half-circle conical roof is often joined to a gable roof shape of equal slope, as in figure 23.1.

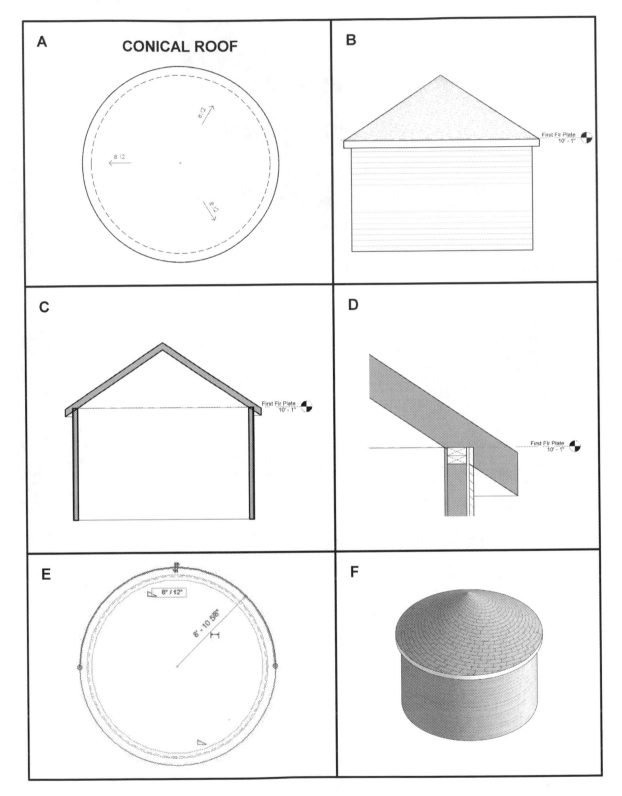

Figure 23.2. Six views of the conical roof

Procedure for Creating a Conical Roof

First we will create the walls for a circular building.

1. In Floor Plan view, start the Wall tool, and set the Top Constraint to be First Floor Plate.
2. In the Draw panel, select the Circle tool.
3. Click a point to become the center of the building. Move the pointer away from the center and you will see a rubber-banding circular wall. Type 8 [ENTER] to set the radius of the wall at 8'0".

Be aware that Revit always splits a 360-degree circular wall into two 180-degree arc-shaped walls.

Next we will model the roof. Go to the Roof Plan view and click on the Roof by Footprint tool. You are now in Sketch Mode. In the Options bar:

1. Ensure that the Defines Slope option is checked.
2. Set the Overhang at 8".
3. Check the Extend to Wall Core option.

Using the Pick Walls tool, click on the upper half-circle wall, making sure that the magenta line is outside of the building. Now click on the lower half-circle wall. You should have two half-circular roof edges forming a circle, as shown in figure 23.2-E.

In the Properties dialog box:

1. Verify that the desired Roof Type is selected.
2. Set the Base Level to First Floor Plate.
3. Verify that the Cutoff Level is set to None.
4. Set the Rafter Cut to Two Cut – Plumb.
5. Set the Fascia Depth to 10".
6. Set the Rafter or Truss setting to Rafter.
7. Change the Slope setting to 8" / 12". Hit the Apply button.
8. Click on the Big Green Checkmark button to accept the sketch and create the roof.

Go to the Default 3-D view. The roof should look like figure 23.2-F.

You will note that the shingles on the roof appear to rise to the top in a spiral pattern. This is true in both 2-D and Realistic view styles. I have not been able to discover why Revit does this. If you prefer to have the shingles level, please refer to chapter 24: "Modeling the Segmented Conical Roof," as well as chapter 26: "Modeling the Onion Dome Roof." The methods used in both of these chapters produce level shingle lines.

Of the three methods, this one is the quickest. If the shingle lines are not an issue, you are done!

Chapter 24

Modeling the Segmented Conical Roof

Figure 24.1. A segmented conical roof on a turret

The segmented conical roof is cone-shaped overall, but a closer look shows that it's made up of many triangular-shaped, flat segments.

The segmented conical roof is created using the same tools as the conical roof. The only difference is the Number of Full Segments setting in the Properties box.

This method has the advantage of making true-level shingle lines (not spiral).

The larger the number of segments you specify, the smoother the shape.

This method can be used for a half-cone shape as well; you simply draw a 180-degree arc instead of a circle.

Procedure for Creating a Segmented Conical Roof

To begin this exercise, follow (or repeat) steps 1 through 7 of the procedure shown in the conical roof in chapter 23. You should now be in Sketch Mode, with two half-circle, magenta-colored roof edges. See figure 23.2-E.

1. Click on the upper half-circle magenta line to select it.
2. Look in the Constraints section of the Properties dialog box and find a setting for Number of Full Segments. See figure 24.2. Change the number to 8 and click on the Apply button.

    Repeat steps 1 and 2 for the lower half-circle magenta edge line.

    Click on the Big Green Checkmark button in the ribbon to accept the sketch.

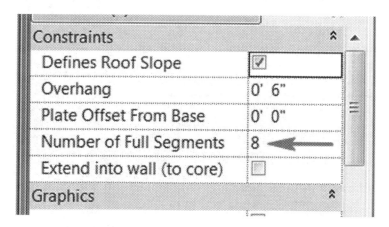

Figure 24.2. Segments setting

You should now have a segmented conical roof similar to the one in figure 24.3. You can use the Linework tool (the hot key is LW) to change the lines between the roof segments to invisible lines if desired, as shown in figure 24.3-F. Notice that the shingle lines are level (not spiraled) using this technique.

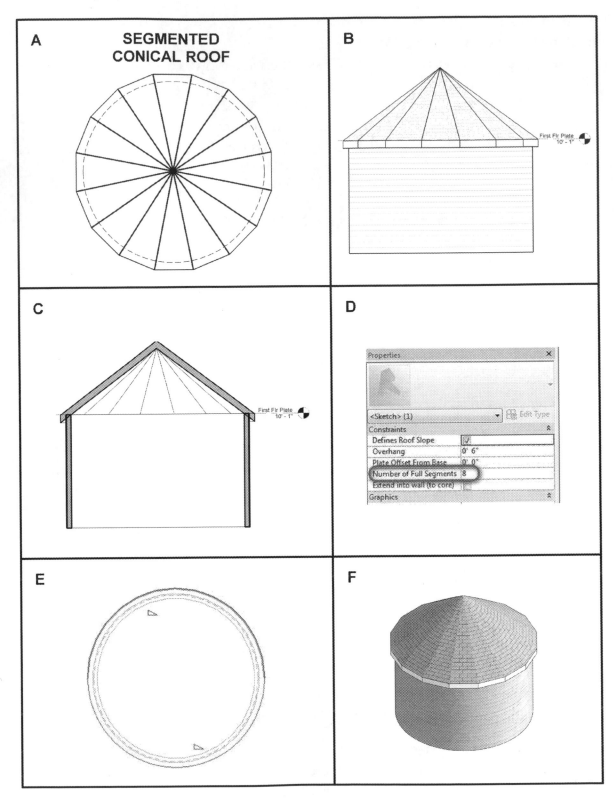

Figure 24.3. Six views of the segmented conical roof

Chapter 25

Modeling the Segmented Dome Roof

Figure 25.1. A segmented dome roof on a turret

A segmented dome roof typically has several sides, and each side has a curving profile that runs in a straight line from one hip line to the next. See figure 25.1 for a great example.

The segmented dome roof is created using the same tools as the swoop part of the bell roof (see chapter 21)—an extruded roof object, trimmed, mirrored, and copied around the central axis.

The profile used for the extrusion can either be curved, as in figure 25.1, or straight.

Our strategy here is to create a roof extrusion in order to give us the general shape of one roof segment and then use the Vertical Opening tool to trim its ends to the proper angle. Lastly, we use the Mirror-Pick Axis tool to mirror it into the final radial arrangement.

Procedure for Creating a Segmented Dome Roof

We will start by making the walls for an octagonal building:

1. In Floor Plan view, create two reference planes that cross each other at what will become the center of the building, one going north to south, the other going east to west.
2. Start the Wall by Footprint (hot key WA) tool.
3. Click on the Circumscribed Polygon tool in the Draw panel.
4. In the Options bar:
   a. Set the Height to be First Floor Plate.
   b. Set the Location Line to be Core Face: Exterior.
   c. Set the number of Sides at 8.

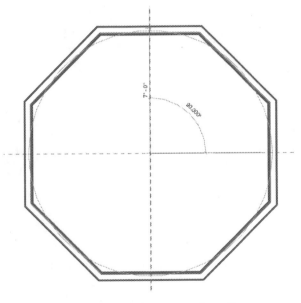

Figure 25.2. Octagonal walls

5. Click a point at the center of the building, and then click another point 7'0" north of the first point. You should now see eight walls in an octagon shape, as in figure 25.2.

This is how we make the roof:

1. Go to the South Elevation view and click on the Roof by Extrusion tool. You'll find it by going to Architecture tab > Build panel > Roof flyout menu > Roof by Extrusion.
2. In the Work Plane dialog box, verify that the "Pick a plane" radio button is selected, click OK to close the box, and get ready to pick the work plane.
3. In the Elevation view, hover over the nearest wall face of the building. Watch for a blue outline to appear around the wall. A tooltip saying "Walls: Basic Wall Exterior etc." should then appear. Click on the wall to select the exterior face of that wall as the Work Plane.

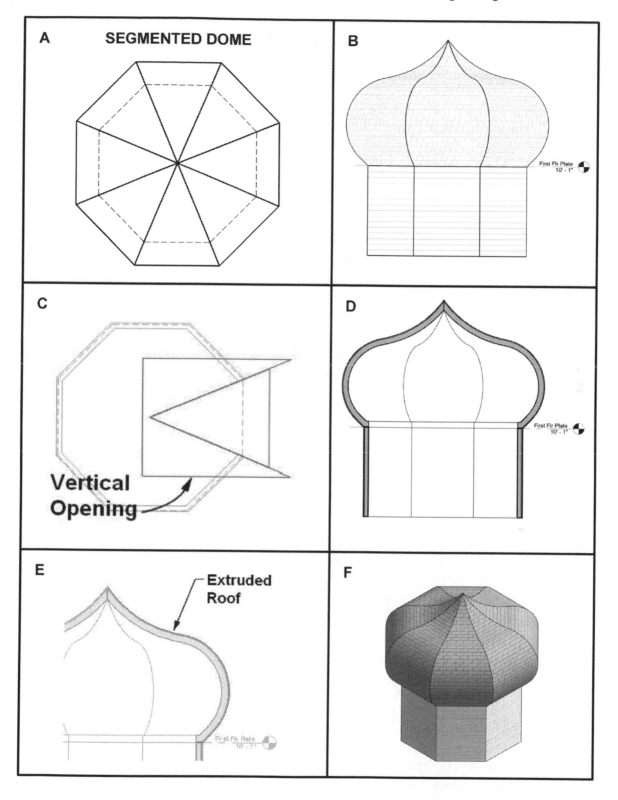

Figure 25.3. Six views of the segmented dome roof

4. The Roof Reference Level and Offset dialog box will appear. For the Level, select First Floor Plate, with an offset of zero. Click on OK. This justifies your roof to the First Floor Plate level. If that level changes height, your roof will move with it.

5. Now you are in Sketch Mode. In the Draw panel, click on the Start-End-Radius Arc tool. Draw a profile similar to the one in View E of figure 25.3-E. This profile can be made of one line or multiple, connecting lines, but it must not be a closed loop. Draw only the exterior surface line of the roof shape.

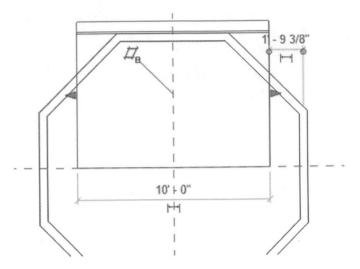

Figure 25.4. The roof extrusion before trimming

6. In the Properties box:
   a. Verify that the Roof Type you want is shown in the Selection Pane of the Properties dialog box.
   b. Set the Extrusion Start value at-2'0". This negative value is measured away from the viewer from the current work plane.
   c. Set the Extrusion End value at-12'0". Again, this negative value is measured away from the viewer.

7. Click the Big Green Checkmark button to accept the sketch and create the first segment's extrusion.

8. Go to the Roof Plan view. Your extrusion should look something like figure 25.4.

Now we will trim the ends of the extrusion to the hip lines.

1. With the roof still selected, click on the Vertical Opening tool in the ribbon.

2. Draw a loop of lines similar to the one shown in figure 25.5-A. The placement of the diagonal lines is critical. Be sure that the first diagonal line extends from the center point of the building to the point where two walls meet, and then stretch it out a short distance beyond the edges of the roof extrusion. Mirror the first diagonal line to make the other diagonal line, using the reference plane as the axis. Everything should center on the intersection of the two reference planes.

3. Click the Big Green Checkmark to accept the sketch and finish the vertical opening. Your roof should now look like figure 25.5-B. This is the first of eight roof segments.

4. While the roof object is still selected, click on Edit Work Plane in the Work Plane panel of the ribbon. In the Work Plane dialog box, click on Dissociate. See figure 25.4-C. I've found this prevents issues later if the roof ever needs moving to a different location.

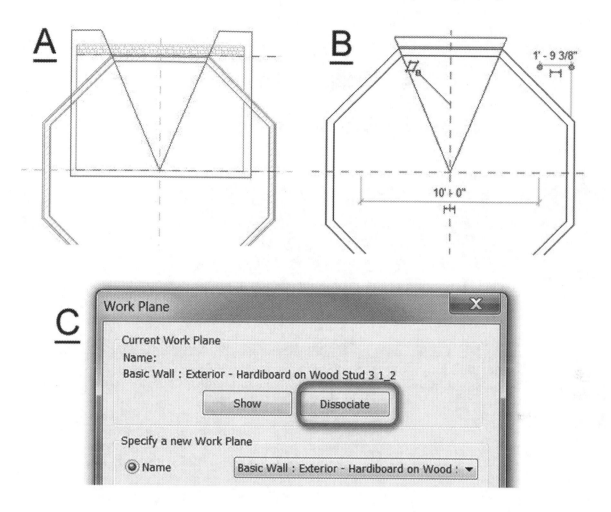

Figure 25.5. Using a Vertical Opening to trim the roof extrusion

5. Use the Mirror – Pick Axis tool to mirror the first roof segment around the entire eight-sided building, using the edge of the roof object itself as the mirror axis.

Your roof should now look similar to the one shown in figure 25.3-F. You're done! This powerful technique can be used for many kinds of polygonal roofs.

Chapter 26

Modeling the Onion Dome Roof

Figure 26.1. A nicely executed example of a revolved-profile dome roof on a turret

The term "onion dome" is being used in this chapter as a kind of shorthand for any roof shape that's created by revolving a two-dimensional profile in a circular path around a vertical axis. The same procedure can be used to create any axially symmetrical, profile-based shape. Aside from true onion-shaped roofs, other possible shapes include a conical roof (which this tool makes with level shingle lines—see chapter 23), a witch's hat roof, or an elliptical dome.

The onion dome roof is created using a Modeled In-Place Family. We select the Roof category to categorize the family, and we use the Solid Revolve tool to create the shape.

The Revolve tool requires that you sketch a profile and designate an axis. Unlike the Roof by Extrusion tool, the profile sketch must be a closed loop of lines, not just the exterior face of the roof.

Procedure for Creating an Onion Dome Roof

First we will create the walls of a circular building.

1. In Floor Plan view, create two reference planes that cross at what will become the center of the building, one going north to south, the other going east to west.
2. Name the two reference planes "Onion CL N–S" and "Onion CL E–W."
3. Start the Wall by Footprint tool.
4. In the Properties box, set the Top Constraint to be First Floor Plate.
5. In the Draw panel, select the Circle drawing tool.
6. Click a point at the intersection of the reference planes. Move the pointer away from the center and you will see a rubber-banding circular wall. Type 8 [ENTER] to set the radius of the walls at 8'0".

The walls are done. The roof is next.

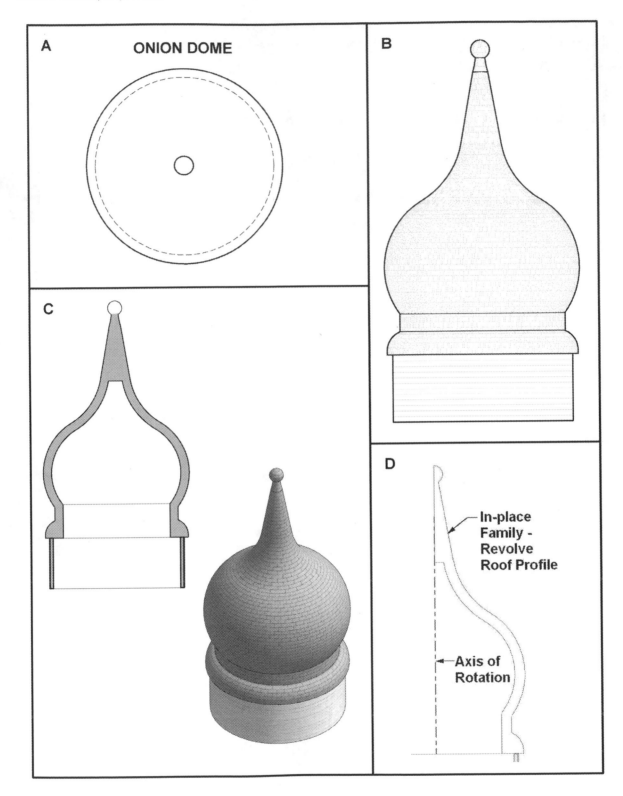

A — ONION DOME

B

C

D — In-place Family - Revolve Roof Profile — Axis of Rotation

Figure 26.2 Five views of the onion dome roof

Now we will create the roof using the Model In-Place tool. Here is the procedure:

1. Go to the West Elevation view of the building. Be sure that the "E-W" reference plane is visible.

2. In the Architecture tab, Build panel, open the flyout menu under Component and select Model In-Place. See figure 26.3-A.

3. In the Family Category and Parameters dialog box that opens, slide down the list and select Roofs. Click on OK.

4. In the Name dialog that opens, type "Onion_1." Click on OK. You are taken to Sketch Mode.

5. In the Create tab > Forms panel, select Revolve. See figure 26.3-B.

6. In the Work Plane dialog that opens, select the Name radio button. Pull down the list next to Name and select the reference plane (from step 5 above) running north to south. See figure 26.3-C. Click OK.

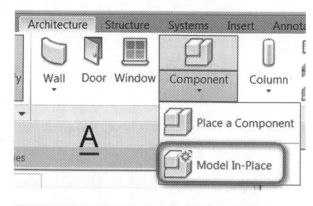

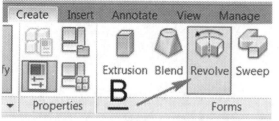

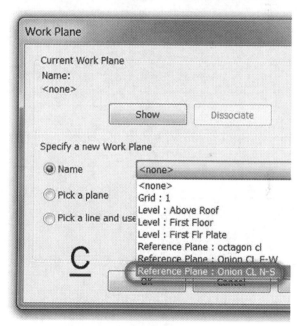

You are now ready to draw the profile. It must be a closed loop of lines. You can make up your own profile or draw one similar to the one shown in figure 26.2-D.

When you've drawn the profile, go to the Draw panel and click the Axis Line button. Now click two points on the East to West reference plane.

Figure 26.3. Beginning the revolve

Click the Big Green Checkmark to accept the sketch.

Go to the Default 3-D view and check your work. If it looks good, click on the Big Green Checkmark button again (this time it's in the In-Place Editor panel) to complete the in-place model.

I have included a dimensioned section view to use if you would like to make a roof like the one shown in this example. Figure 26.4 shows only the exterior face of the profile. Be sure to draw the interior face to make a closed loop of lines, as shown in figure 26.2-D.

Following is a description of how to use these same tools to make a conical roof.

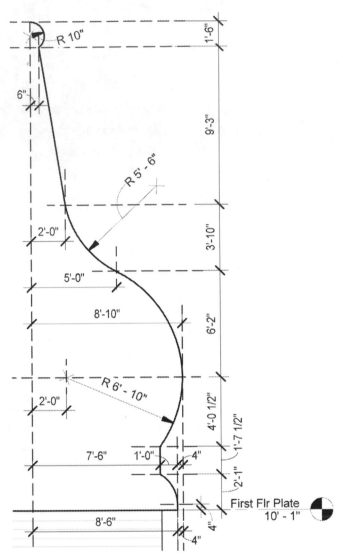

Figure 26.4. Outer onion dome profile

Making a Conical Roof Using a Revolve

You can also use the revolve procedure to create a conical roof. Unlike the spiraling shingle lines we saw on the conical roof we created in chapter 23, the shingle lines come out true-level if we use the Revolve tool. See figure 26.5-A. The profile is shown in figure 26.5-B.

Using the same tools, you can easily make a witch's hat roof. A witch's hat roof typically has a straight upper part and a curved lower part. See figure 26.5-C. The profile I used to create this roof is shown in figure 26.5-D.

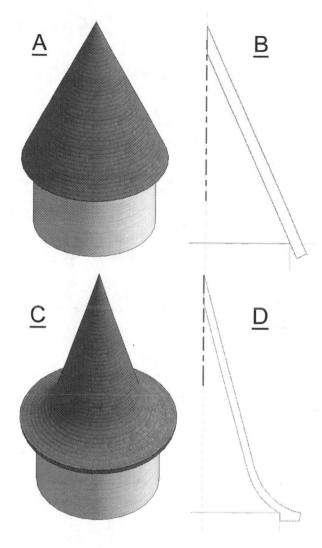

Figure 26.5. Conical and witch's hat roofs

Chapter 27

Manipulating the Gable Roof Shape

Figure 27.1. A contemporary-styled interpretation of a manipulated gable roof

A gable roof shape can be manipulated in many ways in Revit to add interest and cover various room configurations. To explore some possibilities, let's start with one of the oldest traditional roof shapes, the saltbox gable.

Modeling a Saltbox House Roof

The traditional saltbox house has a gable roof with its ridge running left to right, with the entrance on the front and the front wall's top plate higher than the rear wall's upper plate. See figure 27.3-C.

Creating a saltbox house in Revit is easy.

Looking at the house in figure 27.3-C, we see that the front wall extends up to the second-floor plate level, and the rear wall only extends to the first-floor plate level. The challenge is that in Revit, the entire roof must have a single work plane. That means that you cannot justify different roof edge lines to different level data. You must pick one work plane (preferably a level datum) and use it for the entire roof object. Any variation in the heights of the edge lines must be accomplished using Plate Offset from Level settings in the Properties box. These offset dimensions can be positive (up) or negative (down).

Let's make a simple saltbox house. First we set up the levels:

- First Floor at 0'0"
- First Floor Plate Level at 8'0"
- Second Floor Level at 9'0"
- Second Floor Plate Level at 17'0" (9' + 8' ceiling height)

We create four walls with floor plan dimensions of fourteen feet wide by twenty-four feet deep, with the walls justified to the second-floor plate. See figure 27.2-A.

Next, let's set the Work Plane for the roof object. In Modify | Roofs tab > Work Plane panel, click on Set. See figure 27.2-B. In the Work Plane dialog box, from the Name pull-down list, choose Level: Second Floor Plate. Hit OK.

Then we go to Roof Plan view and start the Roof by Footprint tool. Using the Pick Walls tool, with a six-inch overhang, we make four edge lines. The north and south edge lines should be slope defining, with a 9" / 12" slope. The east and west edges should *not* be slope defining.

In the Properties box, change the Fascia Depth setting to 6", and change the Rafter or Truss setting to Rafter. See figure 27.3-A. Hit Apply.

Now we need to calculate the distance from the First Floor Plate to the Second Floor Plate. By subtracting 8' from 17', we find that there is a 9' difference in height between the two levels. This is the magic number to use for our roof offset. Since we justified the roof object to the Second Floor Plate level, the offset required to get down to the First Floor Plate Level at the back wall will be a *negative* nine feet (-9'0").

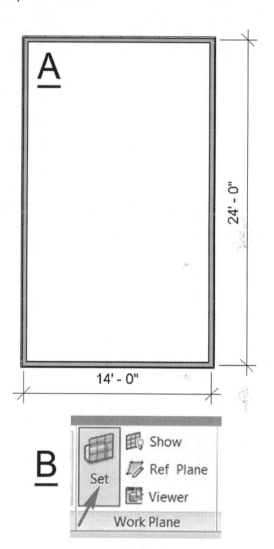

Figure 27.2. Setting the work plane

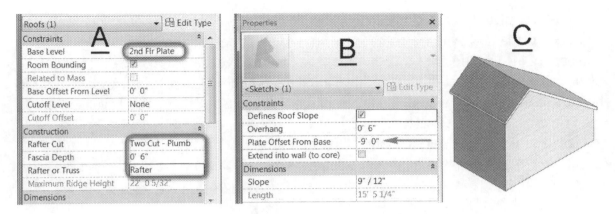

Figure 27.3. Creating a saltbox house

To make this happen, click on the rear (north) edge line and change the Plate Offset From Base setting to negative nine feet (-9'0"). See figure 27.3-B. (The Plate Offset From Base setting of the front [south] edge line should be zero by default.)

Click on the Big Green Checkmark to create the 3-D roof. When Revit asks, "Would you like to attach the highlighted walls to the roof?" choose Yes. In the Default 3-D view, the model should look like figure 27.3-C.

What if you need to create other plate heights in between the two main plate heights? For example, let's make a 6' x 6' offset, or notch, by modifying the walls in the rear part of the plan. See figure 27.4-A.

Next, we will update the roof footprint by selecting the roof in Roof Plan view and clicking Edit Footprint. Modify the footprint to look like figure 27.4-B. Ensure that the new edge lines around the notch are not slope defining. Only the north and south edge lines should be slope defining. Click the Big Green Checkmark and use the Attach Top/Base tool to attach the walls to the roof. The house should now look like figure 27.4-C.

Notice that we do not have to tell Revit how high to make the plate for the non-slope-defining edge next to the notch. It simply falls wherever it falls along the slope of the roof.

After the roof is modeled, we can go to Section view and define the new plate height. We will need this information for the construction documents.

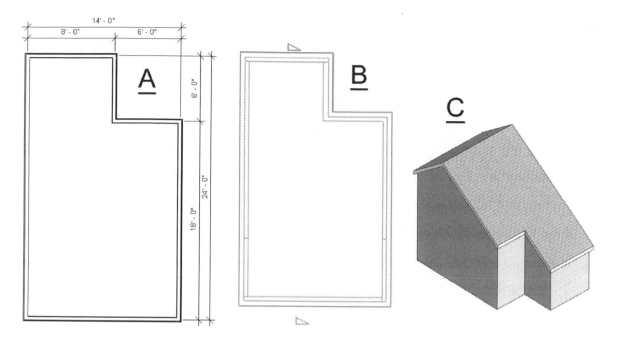

Figure 27.4. A notched-plan saltbox house

Determining the new wall's plate height is not difficult:

1. Turn the Thin Lines toggle to its On position, to make the details easier to see.
2. In Section View, select the wall that's circled in figure 27.5-A. Click on Detach Top/Base button (in the Modify | Wall tab > Modify Wall panel). Now click on the linework of the roof object. The wall should now be detached from the roof.
3. Drag the top of the wall to any random point above the top surface of the roof, using the wall's shape handle. (We do this so that the snap tool can work in the next step.)
4. Draw a horizontal detail line, snapping the first point to the intersection of the interior face of the wall's stud zone with the bottom edge of the roof's rafter zone. See figure 27.5-B. This is the new plate height.
5. Using the Align tool, or simply by dragging the shape handle at the top of the wall, align the top of the wall with the new plate height line.

It's a good idea to create a new level datum and set it to the height of the new plate level. Be sure to create the new level by copying an existing level. Or if you use the Datum > Level button in the ribbon, remember to *uncheck* the setting in the Options bar called "Make New Views." We do not want to add unnecessary junk views in the Project Browser.

Working from a Fixed Ridge Line

What if the design calls for a must-have ridge line location?

Since Revit naturally creates roofs from the bottom edges upward, it is a bit different to work from a fixed ridge line downward and to determine the bearing wall heights.

Figure 27.5-A shows that the current ridge line is 6'0" back from the front wall.

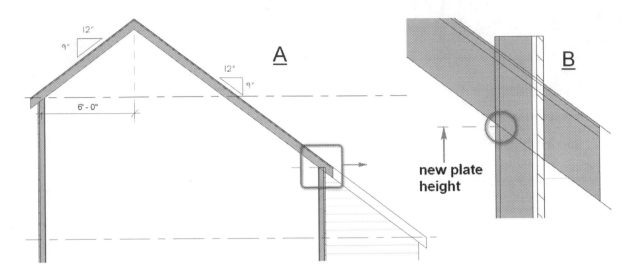

Figure 27.5. Finding the plate height of the new wall

Let's say that for aesthetic reasons, you want to move the ridge line back so that it's exactly 7'0" behind the front wall, measured horizontally. The roof slopes on both faces need to remain at 9" / 12" slope. Let's say further that the front face of the roof will remain justified to the second-floor plate, as it is now, while the top plate heights of the rear walls are allowed to adjust as needed to support the modified rear face of the roof.

One easy way to do this is to split the gable roof into two shed roofs and use a *negative slope* on the rear roof face to work *downward* from the ridge. Yes, Revit does allow you to do that, and often it's a great solution.

Revit allows a negative-slope roof, and this can help you
to work downward from a fixed ridge line.

Continuing with the building that we created in the previous exercise (figure 27.4), we will modify the building as follows:

1. In Roof Plan view, draw a vertical detail line 7'0" back from the front wall. This marks the desired ridge line position. See figure 27.6.
2. Select the roof object and click on Edit Footprint in the ribbon. You are taken to Sketch Mode.
3. Draw a non-slope-defining line across the roof exactly on top of the detail line and trim away or erase all roof edge lines north of that line. See figure 27.7-A. Click on the Big Green Checkmark to approve the sketch.
4. When Revit warns you about "Highlighted walls are attached to, but miss the highlighted targets," click on Detach Target(s). You should now have a building similar to the one in figure 27.7-B.

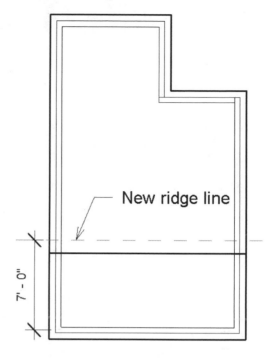

Figure 27.6. Drawing a guide line for the new ridge

We will now build a new shed roof over the rear part of the house. In Roof Plan view:

1. Click on Roof by Footprint. You are taken to Sketch Mode.
2. With the Defines Slope option turned off, and the Overhang still set at 6", using the Pick Walls tool, click on the east, north, and west walls, including the two "notch" walls.
3. Switch to the Line tool in the Draw panel. Turn the Defines Slope option on. Draw a line exactly on top of the new ridge line. Trim the lines as shown in figure 27.7-D.
4. Change the slope for the south edge of the roof (the ridge line) to be *negative* 9" / 12" (-9" / 12"). See figure 27.7-D.
5. Change the Work Plane to Second Floor Plate. (This will be imperfect, but we will fine-tune it later.)

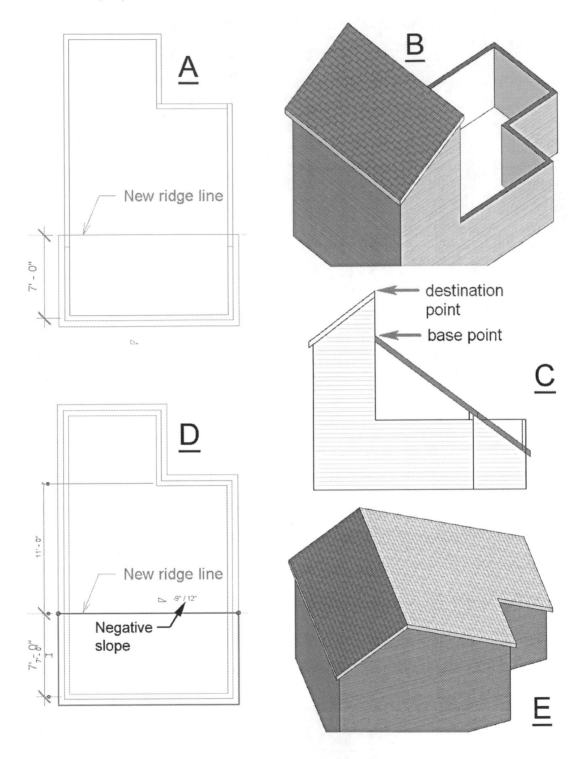

A

New ridge line

7' – 0"

B

destination point

base point

C

D

11' – 0"

New ridge line

-9" / 12"

Negative slope

7' – 8"

E

Figure 27.7. Making a gable roof using two shed roofs meeting at the ridge

6. Click on the Big Green Checkmark. When Revit asks, "Would you like to attach ...," click on Yes.

The roof is created, but it is positioned too low. In Elevation view, using the Move command, raise the rear roof object upward so that the top of the rear shed roof aligns with the top of the front shed roof. See figure 27.7-C.

After attaching all the walls to the new shed roof object, it should look like figure 27.7-E.

The advantage of making a gable roof using two shed roofs, one having a negative slope, is that the back roof of the house can change in many ways (slope, wall position, wall height, etc.) without affecting the front face of the roof or the ridge line.

Chapter 28

How to Make a Cut and Folded Roof

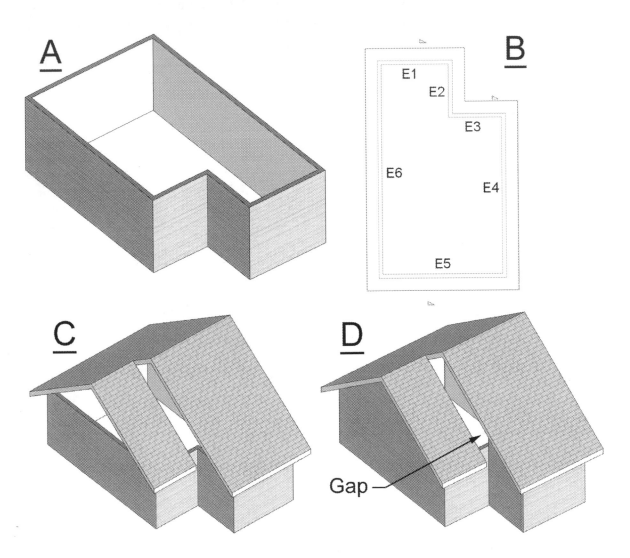

Figure 28.1. Making a cut and folded gable roof

Now we will make a cut and folded roof. This is very easy. We will redo the building we just finished (see figure 27.4) with one simple modification. We will make all three of the east-west-oriented edge lines slope defining and make them all spring from the First Floor Plate level, with no offsets. The result may surprise you!

I'll start by making six walls as shown in figure 28.1-A. All walls should have a Top Constraint of First Floor Plate, with 0'0" Top Offset. The plan dimensions are same as shown in figure 27.4.

Next we will create the roof.

1. Click on Roof by Footprint. You will be taken to Sketch Mode.

2. In the Properties box, change the Base Level of the entire roof to First Floor Plate. Click on Apply.

3. In the Options bar, verify that the Defines Slope option and the Extend to wall core option are checked.

4. Set the Overhang to be 1'6" in the Options bar.

5. Referring to figure 28.1-B, click on the walls labeled E1, E3, and E5 (the slope-defining walls).

6. In the Options bar, now uncheck the box for Defines Slope.

7. Click on edge lines E2, E4, and E6 (the non-slope-defining walls).

8. In the Properties box, change the Rafter or Truss setting to Rafter.

9. Finish by clicking on the Big Green Checkmark button.

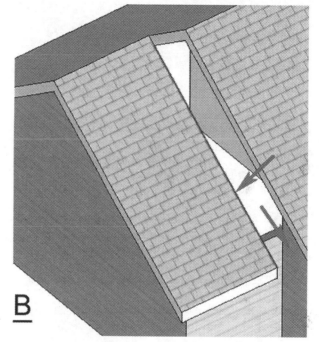

Figure 28.2. Extending a roof to a wall

The roof is created and should look like figure 28.1-C. The roof is cut and folded, and it now has two ridge lines and three faces.

Next we will extend the three east-and-west-facing walls (E2, E4, and E6) to the roof using the Attach to Top/Base tool.

The result is shown below in figure 28.1-D.

This shows that you can easily create a single gable-shaped roof object with more than one ridge. Just create multiple spring points in Plan view for various slope-defining edges.

However, there is a slight issue, which I've indicated with an arrow in figure 28.1-D. We have a gap between the edge of the roof and the infill wall between the upper and lower roof faces.

Fortunately, Revit gives us a great tool to fix this. The Join/Unjoin Roof tool, usually used to join a roof to another roof, can also be used to extend a roof horizontally to a wall. Here are the steps:

1. In Default 3-D view, select the roof object.
2. Click on the Join/Unjoin Roof button (in the Modify | Roofs tab, Geometry panel). See figure 28.2-A.
3. Click on the edge of the roof that needs extending and then click on the wall you want to extend it to. See arrows in figure 28.2-B.

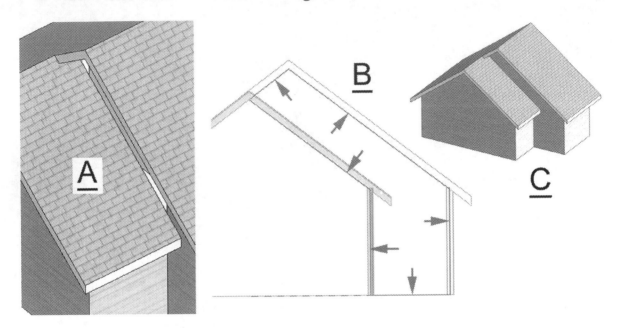

Figure 28.3. Extending the infill wall upward to close the area between roofs

The roof is extended horizontally to meet the wall. See figure 28.3-A.

The next step is to modify the profile of the wall to extend it upward to fill the gap between the upper and lower roofs. Select the wall in Elevation view and use Edit Profile to make the profile look like figure 28.3-B.

Done! Your building should now look like figure 28.3-C. In the next chapter, we will explore another great roof-manipulating tool: the Join/Unjoin Roof tool.

Chapter 29

Using the Join/Unjoin Roof Tool

The Join/Unjoin Roof tool provides an easy way of joining two roof objects. A typical example is a gable-roofed porch roof joining the main hip roof of the house, with their ridge lines perpendicular.

We will show how this works with the following exercise. Start by creating walls as shown in figure 29.1. The porch has three beams, which I modeled using the Wall tool (not the Structural Beam tool). I often use a special wall type (made of solid wood) to model porch beams, partly so that I can use the wall/beam as a justifying element for the roof that bears on it. (You can't justify a roof to a beam in Revit, at least at this time. Also, beams made using the Structural Beam tool are more difficult to edit than my "wall type" beams.)

In figure 29.1, the beams start at 8'0" above the First Floor, and extend up to the First Floor Plate level. The columns go up to 8'0".

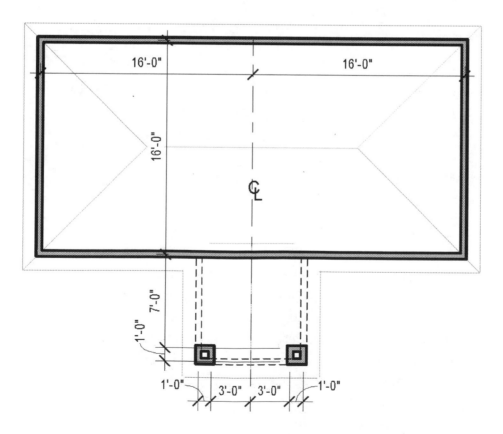

Figure 29.1. Plan of a house with a porch, including dimensions

169

First let's model the hip roof over the house, using the procedure we covered in chapter 13. The overhang dimension will be 1'0" in both the house roof and the porch roof.

Next model a gable roof over the porch area, using the method covered in chapter 12.

The footprint of the roof over the porch should look like figure 29.2-A. Three lines were created using the Pick Walls tool; the fourth line (over the house roof) was drawn with the Line tool. After clicking on the Big Green Checkmark, the roofs should now look like figure 9.2-B.

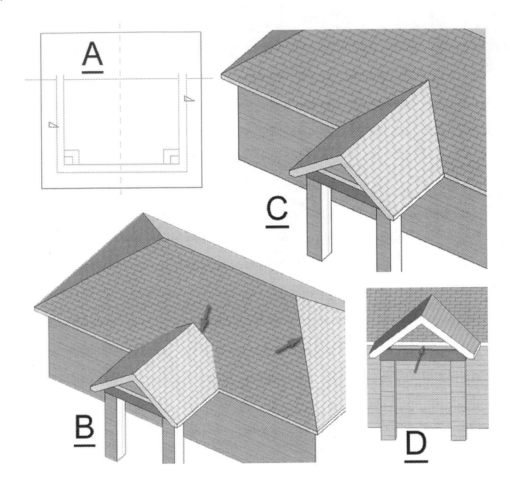

Figure 29.2. Joining two roofs

Now we will join the roofs together using the Join/Unjoin Roofs tool.

Select the porch roof and then click on the Join/Unjoin Roofs button (found in Modify | Roofs tab, Geometry panel). Next, click on the back edge of the porch roof (indicated with an arrow in figure 29.2-B). Finally, click on the large front face of the house's roof—the face that you want the porch roof to be joined to (see the second arrow in figure 9.2-B). Remember that you must click on the linework of the roof object, not somewhere in the interior of the roof face.

The roofs should now be joined, as shown in figure 29.2-C.

There is an issue that arises here. If you orbit around and look under the porch roof, you'll see that the house's main roof has not been modified—it still extends down to the eave line under the porch. This will look problematic in many 2-D and 3-D views. It's best to take a minute and cut away the unwanted roof area under the porch.

There are two ways to do this:

1. Edit the footprint of the house roof, making a notch where the roofs meet; or
2. Use a vertical opening to cut away the unwanted area from the larger roof.

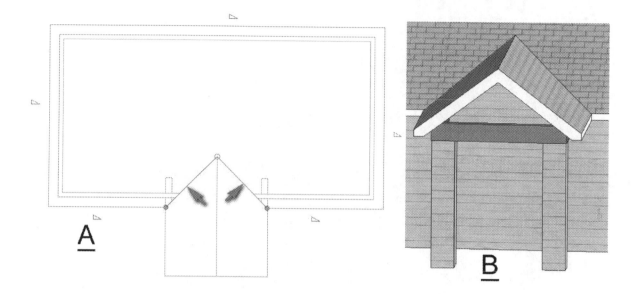

Figure 29.3. Correcting the joined roof's underside appearance

Method 1 is easier—modifying the larger roof's footprint. Go to Roof Plan view and:

1. Select the house roof, and click on Edit Footprint.
2. Make sure that the "Defines Slope" box is unchecked in the Options bar.
3. Use the Pick Lines tool to select the two lines where the porch roof is joined to the house roof (see the arrows in figure 29.3-A). These lines are easy to find, because they were created in the Join/Unjoin Roof action (see figure 29.2-C).
4. Use the Split Element tool (Modify | Roofs tab > Modify panel) to split the south edge line of the house roof, on each side of the porch. Delete the unwanted line segment between the new lines.
5. Trim the corners of the footprint as needed and click the Big Green Checkmark.

Occasionally you may get an error message saying something like "Error – Part of the roof to be joined misses the target face." This means that in some area of the large roof, Revit needs surface area for the small roof to die into, and it's not there. When this happens, I try decreasing the size of the notch where I've removed area from the large roof. This usually silences the error message.

Your roofs are done! Now just extend the wall of the house (under the porch) up to the porch roof by using the Attach Top/Base tool. Don't worry—the wall areas to the left and right of the porch will not be affected by this; only the part of the wall under the porch will be extended upward.

Your porch should now look like figure 29.3-B. Excellent work!

The Join/Unjoin Roofs tool can also be used to join extruded roofs, as shown in figure 29.4. This standing seam metal roof was made using the tools we covered in chapter 14 on barrel roofs.

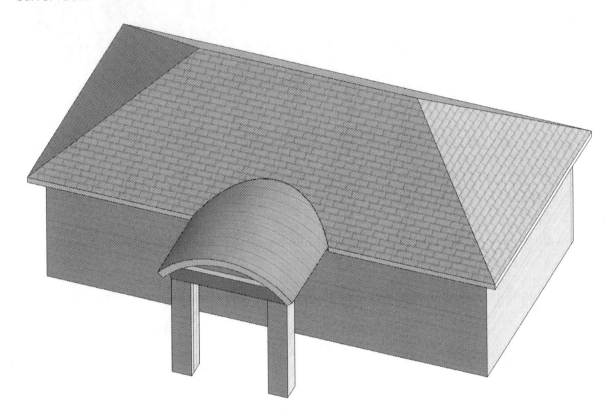

Figure 29.4. A standing seam metal porch roof

Note that if you click this tool once to join two roofs, and then click the roof object a second time, the Roof Join/Unjoin tool becomes an Unjoin tool.

In the next chapter, we will discuss the creation of dormers.

Chapter 30

Dressing Up the Roof With Dormers

Figure 30.1. Dormers can be found in an endless variety of styles

The dormer is one architectural feature where designers really like to show off. Dormers can add a lot to a house design, including balance, proportion, and detail. Sometimes functional, sometimes merely decorative, dormers have a long, rich history and show no signs of going out of style. They are a relatively inexpensive way of gaining light, air, and views and of adding character and interest to the exterior appearance of a house.

Dormers are a bit challenging in Revit, primarily because of their spatial complexity—just like dormers in the real world of construction. Fortunately, Revit has good tools for modeling them.

Dormers can have many shapes, including:

1. Shed roof
2. Gable roof
3. Winged gable roof
4. Hip roof
5. Barrel-shaped roof
6. Eyebrow-shaped roof
7. Half-dormers
8. Recessed dormers

Figure 30.2. A half dormer

A dormer typically has three walls: front, left side, and right side. These walls may go down to the floor, as in a second-floor bedroom, or they may terminate at the roof assembly, as in a high-windowed dormer in a cathedral ceiling, letting daylight into a family room. In the latter case, the side walls are triangular in profile.

Figure 30.3. A gaggle of dormers: barrel, gable, shed, hip, and winged gable

First let's make sure we have our levels set up properly. In a two-story house, the top plate of the dormer's walls may be the same as the second-floor top plate. In this arrangement, the ceiling of the bedroom simply flows into the ceiling of the dormer.

If the house has no rooms on the second floor, and therefore no second-floor plate, the designer will need to create a new level datum for the dormer top plate. You may also want to create a Dormer Plan view, or use a Horizontal Section view, if there is no Second Floor Plan view. Refer to chapter 2, figure 2.6 to see how to create a Horizontal Section view.

In this exercise, I will use the levels below. The Second Floor Plate level will also serve as the dormer walls' top plate level:

- Second Floor Plate: 18'5"
- Second Floor: 10'4"
- First Floor Plate: 9'1"
- First Floor: 0'0"

Critical Dimensions for Dormers

There are two critical dimensions that need to be considered before placing the dormer walls. One is the distance from the first-floor front wall to the front wall of the dormer. It's best to choose this dimension early, since it affects the size and placement of the dormer windows. In this exercise, I used 3'6". See figure 30.4-A. In some houses, this dimension will be zero—the walls of the house and dormer align (see figure 30.2).

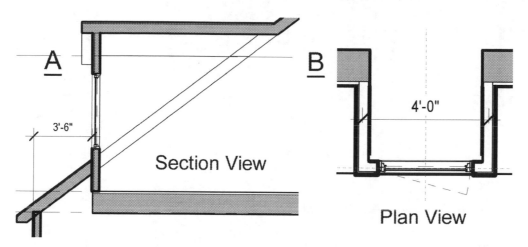

Figure 30.4. Section and Plan view of a dormer

The other critical dimension is the width of the dormer. I made the dormer side walls 4'0" apart (center to center). This allows a dormer window that is 3'0" wide, barely. It's important to leave enough room on the interior side for the window trim to fit between the side walls of the dormer.

Let's open our Second Floor Plan view and begin laying out the dormers.

I created a reference plane 3'6" back from the first floor wall, to mark the location of the front wall of the dormers. See figure 30.4-A.

If the dormer's centerline needs to center on an opening below, I recommend creating a reference plane for the shared centerline of the dormer and the opening below.

The crossing point of these two reference planes is where we locate the center of the front wall of the dormer. See figure 30.5-A, in which the two reference planes are marked with arrows.

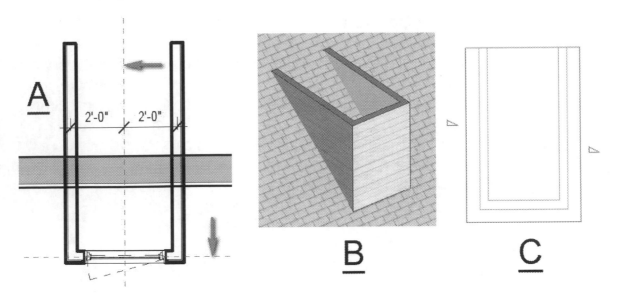

Figure 30.5. Plan and 3-D views of dormer walls

Now we will create the dormer walls:

1. Verify that the Work Plane is set to the Second Floor level. Start the Wall tool.
2. Set the Top Constraint to be Second Floor Plate.
3. Create three walls as shown in figure 30.5-A. The length of the two side walls is just a guesstimate at this point.
4. Check the 3-D view. We want the top edge of the walls to terminate into the roof as shown in figure 30.5-B. Lengthen or shorten the walls as needed.
5. Pop in a window of your choosing, approximately 36" wide by 54" tall. The sill of this window should be at least eight inches above the roof-to-wall intersection (for waterproofing).

We're now ready to make the dormer roof. Go to Roof Plan view. See figure 30.5-C. To make a gable-shaped roof:

1. Start the Roof by Footprint tool. You are taken to Sketch Mode.
2. Set the Base Level at Second Floor Plate (or Dormer Plate, as applies).
3. Set the Overhang to be 9".
4. Click on the three walls, making the edge lines for the two side walls Slope Defining, and making the front edge non–slope defining.
5. Draw a non-slope-defining line using the Line tool across the building side of the roof footprint. Your sketch should look like figure 30.5-C.
6. In the Properties box, change the Rafter or Truss setting to Rafter, and change the Fascia Depth to 5". The Rafter Cut shown here is Two Cut – Plumb.

Click on the Big Green Checkmark to finish the sketch and create the dormer roof.

In the Default 3-D view, extend the front wall up to the roof using the Attach Top/Base tool. Next, attach the dormer roof to the main house roof using the Join/Unjoin Roofs tool (discussed in chapter 29, see figure 29.2). Your roof should look like figure 30.5-A.

The dormer and roof are looking good! However, the main roof is still running through the dormer, and if we look through the window, we can see a shingled roof—not ideal. We need to make a hole in the roof. This is easy using the Dormer Opening tool.

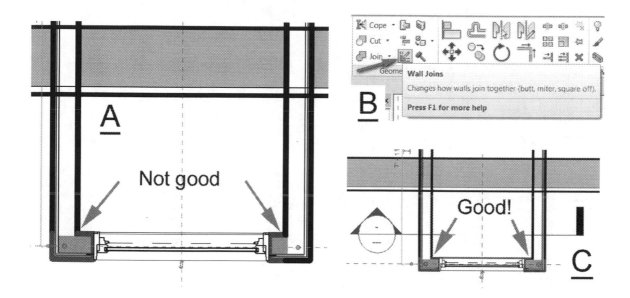

Figure 30.6. Joining the wall corners symmetrically

Using the Dormer Opening Tool

Before we make the opening, we need to head off a potential problem with the sometimes-finicky Dormer Opening tool. At times it refuses to work and gives error messages if the corners of the dormer walls are not joined symmetrically around the dormer's centerline. If they are joined *asymmetrically* (as in figure 30.6-A), Revit may tell you, "Can't create boundary from pick." If you see this error message, go to plan view and use the Wall Joins tool (see figure 30.6-B) to join the walls symmetrically, as shown in figure 30.5-C. Just hover over a wall intersection and use the Next or Previous buttons to select the join type that you want.

The Dormer Opening tool can be a bit finicky at times.

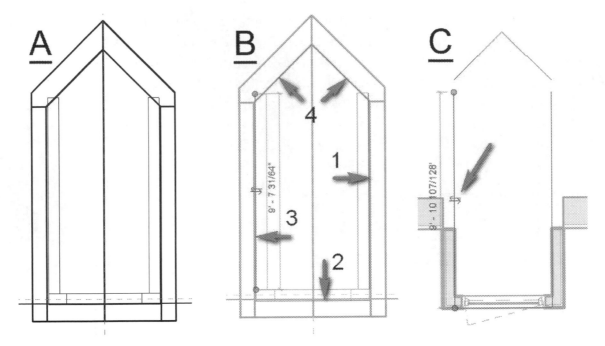

Figure 30.7. Sketching the dormer opening's footprint

Now let's make the dormer opening in the roof. This is really easy:

1. Go to Roof Plan view and change the Visual Style to Wireframe. Your dormer should look something like figure 30.7-A.
2. Click on the Dormer Opening tool (found in the Architecture tab > Opening panel).
3. Click first on the linework of the *main house roof* to select it. This step is easy to overlook, but it is crucial!
4. The numbers in parenthesis () below refer to the numbered arrows in figure 30.7-B:
    a. Click on the line representing the outside of the right side wall (1).
    b. Click on the line representing the outside of the front wall (2).
    c. Click on the line representing the outside of the left side wall (3).
    d. Hover over the dormer roof's linework until it turns blue. Click *once* on the dormer roof, and the two lines at the roof-to-roof connection (marked 4) are created. Remember, only one click is necessary on the roof to form these two lines—and more than one click may cause issues!

Even if the corners appear to need trimming, with the Dormer Opening tool no trimming is necessary. Click the Big Green Checkmark to accept your sketch and make the opening in the roof.

Let's consider which side of the dormer wall—interior or exterior—it's best to select when using the Dormer Opening tool. If your dormer walls extend downward to a floor, as in a second-floor bedroom, it makes sense to terminate the roof at the exterior face of the walls, letting the walls go down to the floor, as we did in the above exercise (see figure 30.8-A).

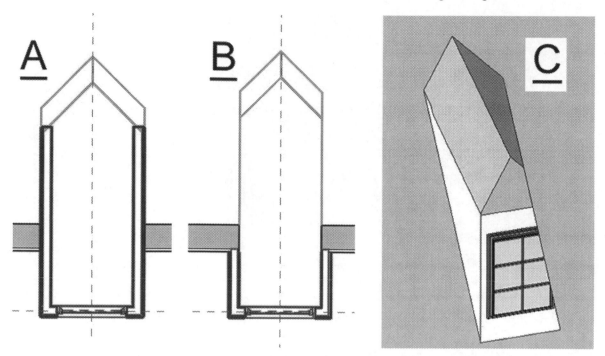

Figure 30.8. Options for the dormer's wall-to-roof connection

On the other hand, if you want a dormer that is open to a double-height space below, as shown in the upward-looking 3-D view in figure 30.8-C, you will probably want the roof opening's edge lines to align with the *interior* side of the dormer walls, as shown in figure 30.8-B. Then you will use the "Base" part of the Attach Top/Base tool to attach the base of the dormer walls to the roof (the "Base" option radio button is found in the Options bar).

You can change your decision on this after the dormer opening is created. See figure 30.7-C. If you go back to the Second Floor Plan view and hover over the opening's edges, the edges appear in blue, with a tooltip saying "Roof opening cut: Dormer opening." Hit Tab a time or two if needed. Click on the opening outline when you see it, and you get a double blue arrow symbol (see the arrow in figure 30.7-C). By clicking the double blue arrow, you can toggle the edge line from interior face to exterior face.

I used the Geometry > Join tool to join the dormer walls to the main house roof/ceiling assembly in figure 30.8-C. This tool does a good but not perfect job of getting rid of the lines where the objects meet. Sometimes the joint lines appear dotted. The Linework tool does not recognize lines between joined objects, so that tool is not useful for this issue. There's room for some improvement in the Geometry Join tool.

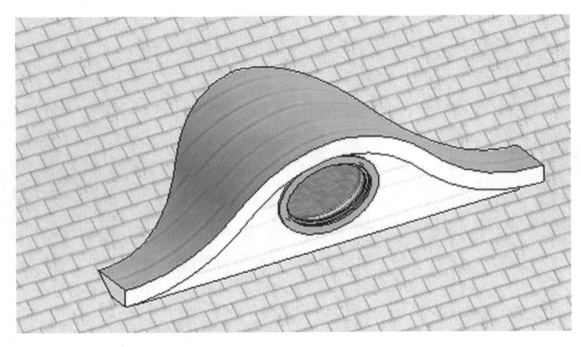

Figure 30.9. An eyebrow dormer created using the Roof by Extrusion tool

All of the dormer shapes listed at the start of this chapter can be modeled using the methods we described. The various roof shapes can be found in the Basic Roof Shapes part of the book (chapters 10–26). The eyebrow dormer in figure 30.9 was modeled using the Roof by Extrusion tool and joined to the main house roof using the Roof Join/Unjoin tool.

The dormer possibilities in Revit are endless!

Chapter 31

Soffits and Eave Terminations

Figure 31.1. A hip-shaped shingled eave return on a gable roof

Eaves have many kinds of terminations. Here we will look at creating soffits, bird boxes, and shingled eave returns.

While bird boxes are traditionally built to keep birds from nesting under an eave, sometimes they are actually built with openings for birds to come in and make themselves a home.

A bird box is also useful for providing a graceful way of terminating a soffit when it reaches a gable end. We'll start by making a soffit for a storage building and see how this works.

Figure 31.2. A bird box detail

Let's start with a small 12' x 10' building, say a storage building. The building is shown in figure 31.3. The overhangs for the north, west, and south edges is 1'6". The overhang for the east (front) side is 1'0". The Rafter Cut shape is Two Cut-Plumb, and the Fascia Depth is 6". Go ahead and create the roof.

Creating a Soffit

Here's the procedure for making a soffit:

1. Go to Roof Plan view and change the Visual Style to Wireframe.
2. Set the Work Plane to be First Floor Plate.
3. Click on Architecture tab > Build panel > Roof flyout menu > Roof Soffit. You are taken to Sketch Mode.

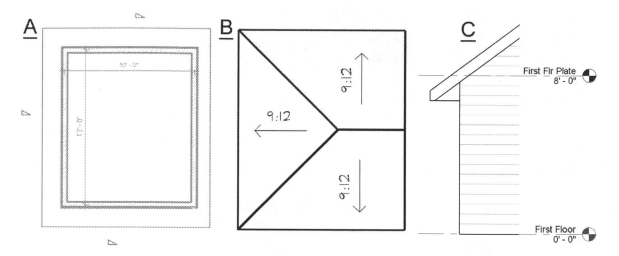

Figure 31.3. Making the storage building's roof

4. In the Draw panel, select the Pick Roof Edges tool and then hover over the linework (anywhere) of the roof object. The linework turns blue. Click on the roof object. The roof is selected and turns blue. Move the pointer away and look close—there are magenta lines overlaid on some of the blue lines. These are the outer edges of your soffit.

5. Click on the Pick Walls tool in the Draw panel. Click on the north, west, and south walls. Magenta lines appear on the exterior edge lines of these three walls.

6. Click on the Line tool in the Draw panel. Draw two short lines to close off the ends of the loop. Align these two short lines with the front (east) face of the building wall.

7. Trim the corners of the footprint as needed. See figure 31.4-A.

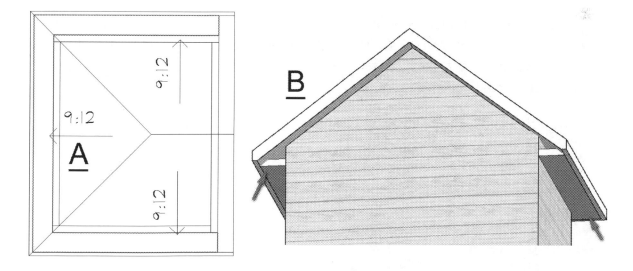

Figure 31.4. Making the roof soffit

8. Click on the Big Green Checkmark. The soffit is created but is too high.
9. Go to the Elevation view and use the Align tool (hot key is AL) to align the bottom edge of the roof with the bottom edge of the soffit (see figure 31.4-B).

Your soffit is done. Now we need to look at the terminations. First we will add bird boxes.

Creating a Bird Box

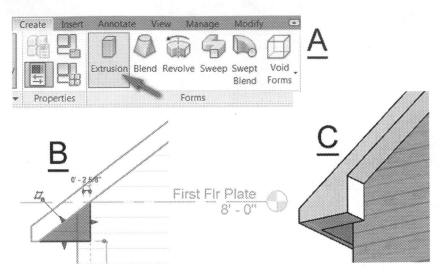

Figure 31.5. Making a bird box

We will now create the left bird box, using the Model In-Place tool to create a solid extrusion.

1. Go to the East Elevation view.
2. Click on Architecture tab > Build panel > Component flyout menu > Model In-Place.
3. For the Family Category, choose Roofs.
4. For the Name, type "Bird Box 1."
5. Click on Create tab > Forms panel > Extrusion (see figure 31.5-A).
6. The Work Plane dialog box opens. Choose Pick a plane and click OK.
7. Hover over the front (east) wall of the building. When its outline glows blue, click.

You are taken to Sketch Mode. Next:

1. Draw a triangle as shown in figure 31.5-B.
2. In the Properties box:
   a. Change the Extrusion End setting to 1'0".
   b. Verify that the Extrusion Start setting is 0'0".
   c. Change the material as desired. I usually use White Plastic, which resembles a white-painted wood, until I know the final material.

3. Click on the Big Green Checkmark again.
4. Use the Geometry > Join tool to join the bird box to the roof object. See figure 31.5-C.

The bird box can now be mirrored over to the right side of the gable roof and joined to the roof there. It can also be copied into a different work plane for use on a different face of the building. In order to be able to copy it to a different work plane, I follow this procedure:

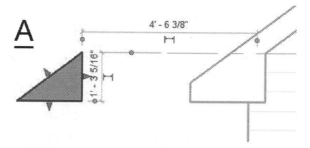

1. In elevation, select the first bird box and click on Copy (hot key CC). Copy it outside of the building elevation linework (see figure 31.6-A).
2. Select the copied bird box and click on Modify | Roofs tab > Model panel > Edit In-Place. You are taken to Sketch Mode.
3. Select the floating bird box again and click on Modify | Extrusion > Work Plane panel > Edit Work Plane button.
4. The Work Plane dialog box opens. Click on the Dissociate button (See figure 31.6-B).

Figure 31.6. Dissociating a work plane

Go to Roof Plan view. The bird box is now free to be moved in any direction and rotated as needed. Once in place in a different gable, it can be stretched using its shape handles.

Creating a Shingled Eave Return

A shingled eave return is simply a very small hip or shed roof used to fill in the space at the termination of the eave of a gable roof. Typically it is built to look as if it flows continuously into the gable roof. Sometimes it's just called a *return*, a *box return*, or a *cornice return*.

We will use the same storage building we created in the previous exercise. Just copy the entire building and delete the bird boxes.

The return will be modeled as a separate roof object and then joined to the main roof.

In Roof Plan view:

1. Draw two detail lines, 1'9" apart, as shown in figure 31.7-A.
2. Click on Roof by Footprint.
3. In the Options bar, set the Overhang at 1'6", and check the Defines Slope box.
4. In the Properties box, set the Base Level to First Floor Plate.
5. Verify that the Pick Walls tool is selected.
6. Click on the east wall and the south wall of the building. You should now see two magenta lines. Trim these two magenta lines as shown in figure 31.7-A.
7. Select the shorter magenta line and mirror it to the north, using the first detail line as the mirror axis. See figure 31.7-B. Extend this line to the building wall as shown.
8. Uncheck the Defines Slope box in the Options bar and draw three non-slope-defining lines, as indicated with arrows in figure 31.7-C. The second line should have an angle of exactly forty-five degrees from the roof edge line.

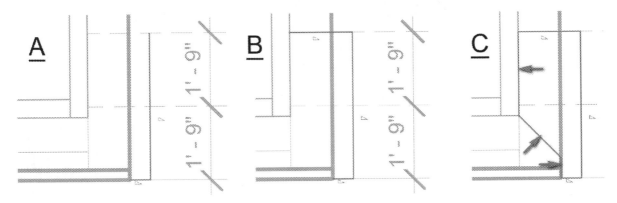

Figure 31.7. Sketching the eave return's fo

Click on the Big Green Checkmark. You have created a shingled hip return, but it still needs a bit of adjustment.

In Elevation view:

1. With the return object selected, change the Fascia Depth setting to 6".
2. Move the shingled return object downward so that the eave of the return aligns with the eave of the main roof.

Your return should now look like figure 31.8-A. All that remains is to extend the footprint of the soffit so that it fills the underside of the return. See figure 31.8-B.

This same method can be adapted to make a shed-roof-shaped return, as opposed to the hip-roof-shaped return above. Below is the procedure to make a shingled shed return.

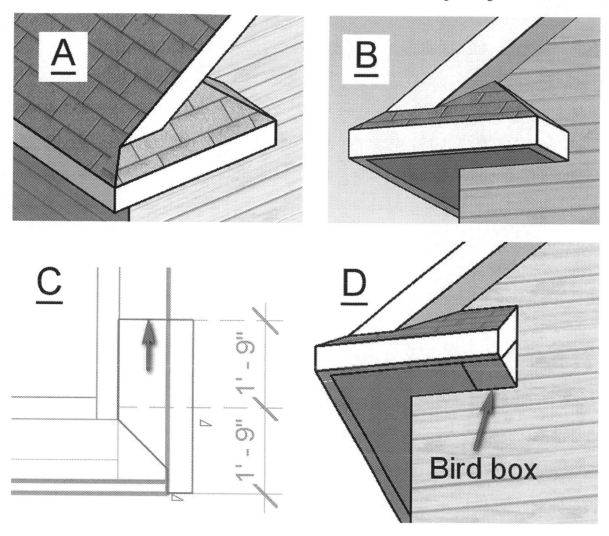

Figure 31.8. Hip-roof-shaped and shed-roof-shaped eave returns

Make the return in the same way as shown in figure 31.7, but while you're in Edit Footprint mode, make the north edge line (indicated with an arrow in figure 31.8-C) *non–slope defining*. Click the Big Green Checkmark to finish the model. Then take a copy of the bird box that we modeled earlier (see figure 31.5) and move it into position at the end of the new fascia, as shown in figure 31.8-D. Join the bird box object to the roof, using Geometry > Join. Done!

Don't forget to dissociate the work plane of the bird box model (see figure 31.6), so that you will be able to rotate it into this position. You are now a master of the bird box!

The Power of Slope Arrows

Figure 32.1. The two small gable roofs can be modeled easily using slope arrows

Slope arrows in Revit are an alternative to slope-defining edges, with extra "powers" that slope-defining edges lack. Like slope-defining edges, they can give a slope to any roof object. They can also make a roof soffit or a ceiling slope. They have additional flexibility beyond that offered by slope-defining edges. For example, if you want a sloping roof to rise exactly two feet over some unknown horizontal distance, regardless of its slope ratio, it's easy to do that with a slope arrow.

Slope arrows can control a roof's slope in either of two ways:

- Specify Slope, in which the designer specifies the slope ratio and the height of the beginning point, based on the roof's level and (optionally) an offset up or down.
- Specify Height at Tail, in which the designer specifies the height of the roof at the beginning points and endpoints of the arrow, based on levels and (optional) offsets.

I think of these as two separate modes of operation, producing totally different results.

189

Slope arrows can create a slope in any direction. For example, a rectangular roof object can slope diagonally from a corner to the opposite corner by using a slope arrow.

A slope arrow can create a rake edge on a roof without having a perpendicular slope-defining edge at the bottom of the slope. See figure 32.1.

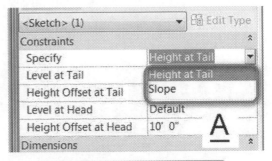

The Slope Arrow tool can only be seen when you are in Edit Footprint (Sketch) mode (see the twin gables in figure 32.3). Your first click point becomes the Tail, and the second click point becomes the Head.

It took me a while to figure out that:

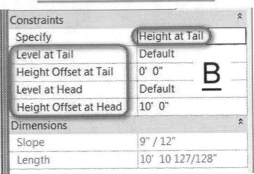

- The "Tail" is the endpoint of the slope arrow that does *not* have an arrowhead shape. We will call this the "Tail Point," which I think makes it easier to understand.
- The "Head" is the end point of the slope arrow that *does* have an arrowhead shape. We will call this the "Head Point."

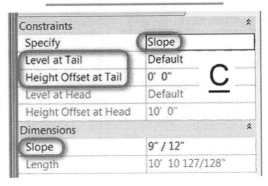

The two modes of Slope Arrow operation are called:

1. Specify Height at Tail, or
2. Specify Slope

The following discussion will help clarify how each of these works.

Figure 32.2-A shows the pull-down menu where you can select one of the two modes. Specify Height at Tail is the default setting.

Figure 32.2. Specify options for slope arrow

Figure 32.2-B shows the appearance of the property box if you choose Specify Height at Tail mode. I've circled the options that you can set in this mode; the other options are grayed out and cannot be selected. You can set the level at the tail point and an offset (if desired) from that level.

"Default" in this case means the level of the edge derived from the Base Level setting of the overall roof object, and the Overhang setting of the edge line. You can also set the level at the Head Point and any desired offset. These four settings control the heights of the start point and endpoint of the sloping surface controlled by the slope arrow. The slope ratio is whatever it works out to be.

Figure 32.2-C shows the property box if you choose Specify Slope mode. In this mode, you set the level at the Tail Point and an offset from that level (if desired), and then you specify the slope ratio.

Rules of Slope Arrows

Slope arrows have some peculiar rules, including:

1. You can have multiple slope arrows on one object.
2. You can have both slope arrows and slope-defining edges in one object.
3. The *Tail Point* of any slope arrow must lie on a roof boundary line.
4. The *Head Point* of a slope arrow can lie anywhere, inside or outside of the roof boundary.

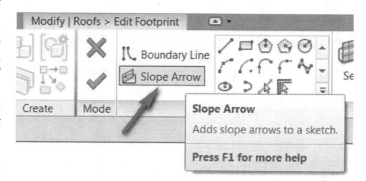

Figure 32.3. Slope Arrow button

5. The Tail Point of a slope arrow must not lie anywhere "in the middle" of a slope-defining edge (that is, between its endpoints). However, it *can* lie on an endpoint of a slope-defining edge.
6. If you use the Specify Slope mode, it doesn't really matter where you locate the Head Point; what matters is the direction of travel from the Tail Point to the Head Point.
7. If you use the Specify Height at Tail mode, it *does* matter where you place the Head Point. The Head Point's location is where the arrow's specified height is reached (or would be reached, if it does not collide with another slope first). After that point, the slope either continues to the opposite edge of the roof, or it continues until it collides with another slope, forming a ridge or hip line.

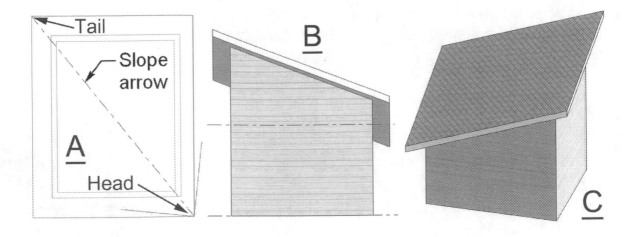

Figure 32.4. A roof made to slope corner to corner, using a slope arrow

Let's show how this works with the creation of an actual roof.

Using Slope Arrows

Using the storage building from the previous chapter, I went to Roof Plan view. I made all the edges non–slope defining.

Then I drew a slope arrow from the top left corner to the bottom right corner, as shown in figure 32.4-A. The result is shown in figure 32.4-B (an Elevation view) and figure 32.4-C (3-D view). You can choose either Mode of Operation for the slope arrow in this example.

To show another example of the power of the slope arrow, I'll make a square 12' x 12' building and use slope arrows to make a sort of facet-shaped roof, a rotated hip roof with four diamond-shaped gable sides.

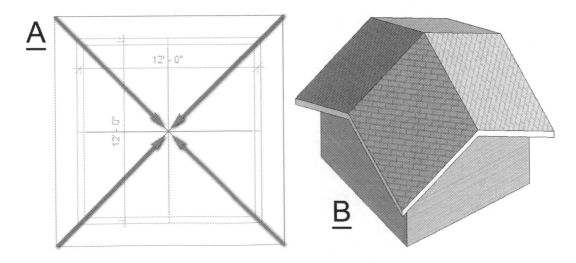

Figure 32.5. Four slope arrows make a unique, faceted roof shape

Start with a square roof footprint with no slope-defining edges and then add four slope arrows as shown in figure 32.5-A (I've drawn my own thick graphic arrows over the Revit arrows for clarity.) These slope arrows are set to Specify Slope mode with a 9" / 12" slope setting. The resulting roof shape is shown in figure 32.5-B. Notice that there are no slope-defining edges in this roof.

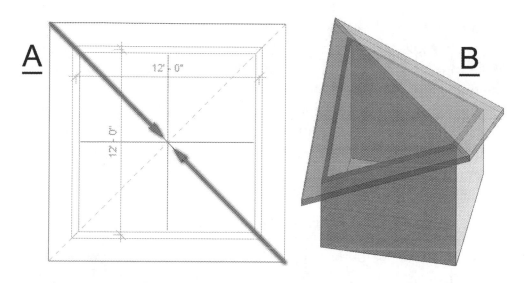

Figure 32.6. A birdlike corner-to-corner ridge shape

Take away two of the slope arrows, leaving only two remaining, and you get the roof shown in figure 32.6, with a diagonal ridge line.

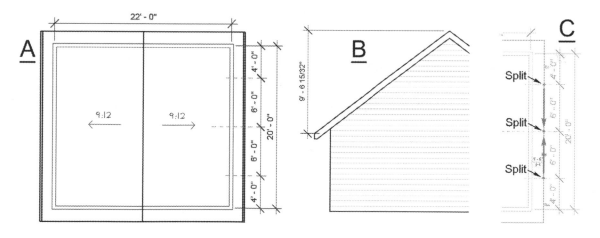

Figure 32.7. Start with a simple gable

Creating an Intersecting Gable

Now let's make a roof similar to one of the twin gables in figure 32.1. Start with a 22' x 20' rectangular plan as shown in figure 32.7-A. Using the Roof by Footprint tool with a 1'6" overhang, create a gable roof with slope-defining edges on the east and west sides of the house.

Draw three reference planes as shown, which will mark the sides and centerline of the small intersecting gable. Now, using the Split tool, split the east edge line as shown in figure 32.7-C. Make the two line segments between the split points non–slope defining while leaving the two outside line segments slope defining.

Next, draw two slope arrows as shown in figure 32.7-C. Make the slope arrows in Specify Slope mode, with a 16" / 12" slope. After clicking the Big Green Checkmark, the result is shown in figure 32.8-A. This looks very much like one of the two intersecting gables in the photo at the beginning of this chapter.

Now, to show the power of the Specify Height at Tail mode of the slope arrow tool, let's say you want to make the ridge line of the intersecting gable align perfectly with the ridge of the main house roof, regardless of the slope ratio of the intersecting gable roof. This is easily accomplished using Height at Tail mode.

Using the roof project we just completed, go to Edit Footprint mode and select the two slope

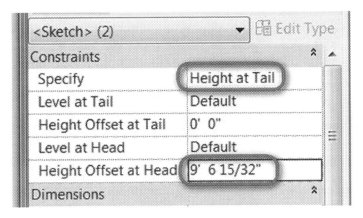

Figure 32.8. Settings for new roof

arrows. As shown in figure 32.8, change the Specify setting to be Specify Height at Tail mode. Make the Height Offset at Head setting for the two slope arrows match the vertical height from the eave line to the ridge line of the house roof, as shown in figure 32.7-B. In my project, that dimension happened to be 9'6 15/32". Click on Apply and the Big Green Checkmark. The resulting roof is shown in figure 32.9-B, with the two ridge lines aligning perfectly.

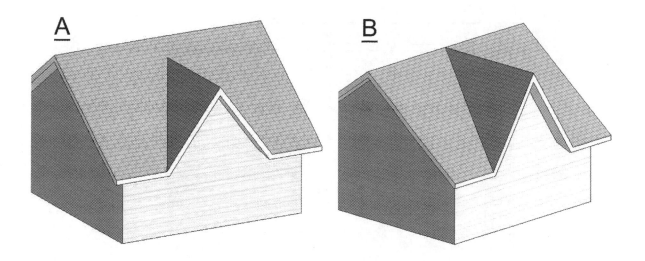

Figure 32.9. Slope arrows can control either the slope or the roof's overall height

If you want to find out the slope of the intersecting gable, just go to the Annotate tab and use the Spot Slope tool on the Roof Plan view. See figure 32.10-A. You can change the Units Precision setting by selecting any Spot Slope arrow object and going to Type Properties > Units Format (see figures 32.10-B and 32.10-C). The slope of the intersecting gable is shown to be 19" / 12".

As we've seen, the slope arrow is a very powerful tool—actually, two powerful tools in one. It is definitely worth adding to your Revit roof design toolbox.

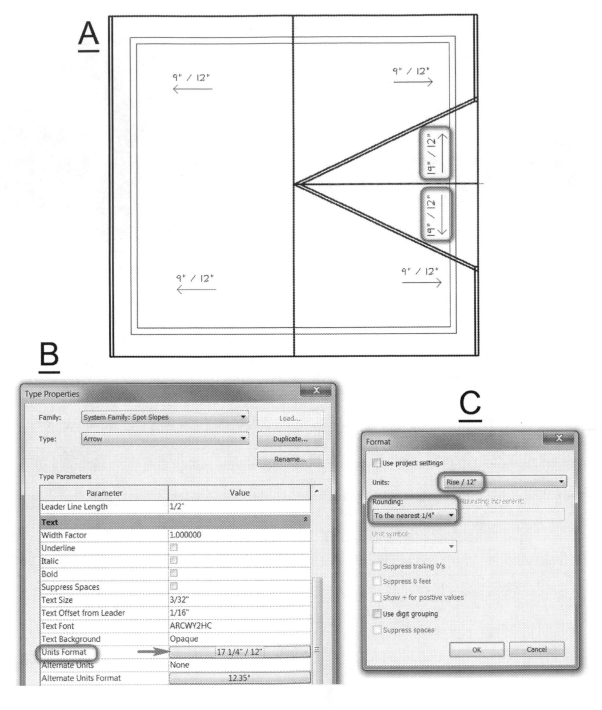

Figure 32.10. Controlling the spot slope units formatting

Putting It All Together

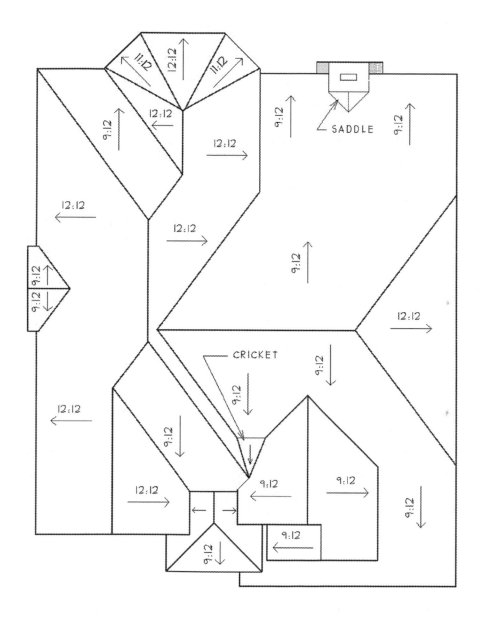

Figure 33.1. Roof Plan for modeling exercise

Now let's take several of the methods we've covered and use them to model a fairly complex house roof.

Most custom houses today require multiple roof objects to cover the various shapes of the rooms. Knowing how to divide a roof into separate roof objects, or what I call *chunks*, is key to efficient roof modeling in Revit. I call this process the *chunking down* of a roof.

197

One rule of thumb for roof chunking is that if part of a roof passes underneath another roof, so that the lower roof is in the higher roof's shadow, it's likely that you will need to model the roofs as two separate objects. There are exceptions, however—see figure 28.3, where we extended a roof horizontally to terminate against a wall. In general, however, a Revit roof object cannot pass below itself—that is, it cannot cast a shadow on itself.

With few exceptions, a single Revit roof object cannot pass
beneath itself, so as to cast a shadow on itself.

On the other hand, when two or more parts of a roof share a continuous eave, there is a good chance that they can be modeled as a single object. It's sometimes, but not always, faster to model a roof using fewer objects rather than working out the joining issues on a large number of roof parts.

It's a good idea to plan your strategy before beginning a roof-modeling project. I always try to determine all the plate heights I will need and create additional level data if needed. I make sure I know the overhang dimensions that are wanted and the desired shape of the rafter tails (for more on this, please refer to chapter 5). If the design calls for bastard hips, I determine whether using different overhangs on the two sides of the hip line is acceptable (see chapter 22). In this example, I decided that the overhang dimensions could vary, hence my use of the Align Eaves > Adjust Overhangs option.

Figure 33.1 shows the roof plan of a two-story house with multiple shapes. We will use it as an example of chunking a roof into multiple objects. First let's consider how to divide the roof into manageable parts. In figure 33.2, each of the shaded areas is a chunk.

Figure 33.2-A is a hip roof shape, and it has bastard hip lines because of the different slopes it contains. The east and west faces have a 12" / 12" slope, while the north and south faces have 9" / 12" slope. To make the eaves align in elevation, I used the Align Eaves tool with the Adjust Overhang option (see chapter 22). The rear (north) overhang came out wider (1'4") than the side overhang (1'0"). This roof object bears on the second floor's top plate.

The next chunk—figure 33.2-B—is over the east part of the house. Its shape is a half-hip, which we covered in chapter 17. The plate height for the east edge of the roof footprint was offset upward by 9'0", to match the distance from the first floor plate up to the second floor plate.

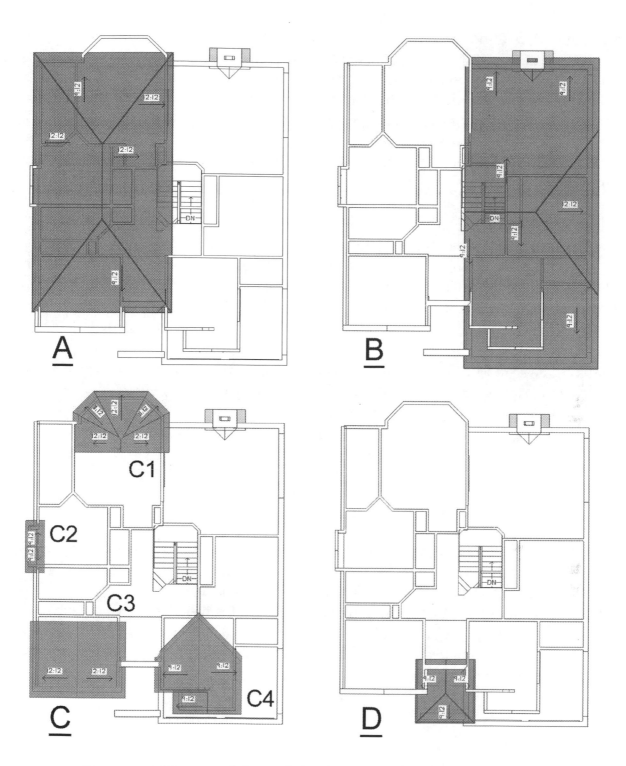

Figure 33.2. Diagram of the roof chunks used in this chapter's exercise

Figure 33.2-C shows four more chunks: C1, C2, C3, and C4.

Chunk C1 is a modified hip roof that follows the bay shape of the walls below. While the main slope of this roof object is 12" /12", the northeast and northwest roof faces had to be sloped at 11" / 12" to make all the hip lines meet at the apex. I determined the 11" / 12" slope ratio simply by experimenting with different ratios until it came out right. Nothin' fancy. Of course, this created misaligned eaves in elevation, due to the bastard hip conditions where the different slopes meet. I corrected these using the Align Eaves > Adjust Overhangs tool (see chapter 22).

Chunk C2 is a simple gable roof over a bumped-out bathroom. Easy. See chapter 12 for discussion of the gable roof.

Chunk C3 is a simple gable roof over a bedroom.

Chunk C4 is a cut-and-folded gable roof, like we discussed in chapter 28. I used the Join/Unjoin Roof tool to extend the lower roof horizontally to meet the nearby wall, as shown in figure 28.2-A. This tool is a bit finicky about the profile of the wall that you are attaching the roof to. I got the "The roof cannot be joined" error message. By using Edit Profile > Reset Profile tool on the wall, and experimenting with the wall shape, I was able to make it work. The wall must be not too short and not too tall, or you get error messages. It might be easier to simply create two gables and join them using Geometry > Join.

Chunk 33.2-D is a simple hip roof, cut off straight on the side facing the house. Its spring line is a few feet lower than the second-floor top plate, so I created a new level datum for the plates that this roof object bears upon. Easy.

Joining the Various Roof Chunks

Figure 33.3 shows the roof before the chunks were joined together. Some of the chunks overlap, and some stop short of the intended termination with other roof faces. Joining the chunks together was not difficult. I'll discuss each join separately.

I joined Chunk B to Chunk A by using the Join-Unjoin Roofs tool (see chapter 29).

Chunk C1 refused to be joined to Chunk A using the Join/Unjoin Roof tool. This was possibly due to the complexity of C1's shape. Therefore I went to my second choice, the Geometry > Join tool, to merge the two roof objects. This tool worked like a charm.

Chunks C2 was joined to Chunk A using the Join/Unjoin Roof tool.

Chunk C3 was joined to Chunk A using the same method. I joined Chunk C4 to Chunk B the same way.

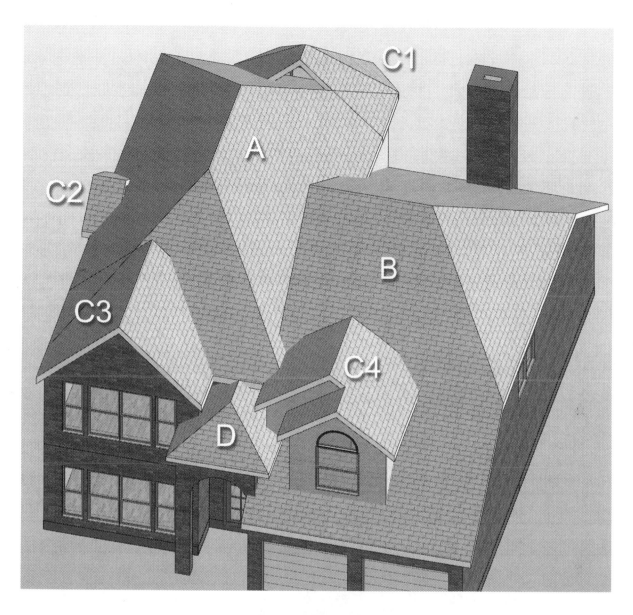

Figure 33.3. The roof chunks before joining

Chunk D's footprint was adjusted using Edit Footprint to meet the walls properly.

The results are shown in figure 33.4. Notice that the "extra" lines where one object overlaps or intersects another object are gone. All the joins are clean. Success!

Figure 33.4. The roof chunks after joining—front bird's-eye view

All that remains is to add the trim, if desired. This might include soffits, fasciae, gutters, eave returns, bird boxes, crickets, and saddles. A cricket is just a tiny shed roof cut to a triangle and sloped using a slope arrow. A saddle is a small gable roof built on the uphill side of the chimney to divert rainwater to each side. See figure 33.1 for the locations of the cricket and saddle in this project. Soffits, bird boxes, and eave returns were discussed in chapter 31.

Remember that when two roof objects overlap, and the faces of the two roof objects are perfectly coplanar, you can use the Geometry > Join tool to convert the roof objects into a single object, thereby eliminating the telltale edge lines at the overlapped area.

You now know all the pieces that can be put together to make a house roof. You also know various ways of putting them together effectively and efficiently. And by using Revit's capabilities, you are creating the 3-D roof, the perspective views, and all of the associated 2-D views at the same time!

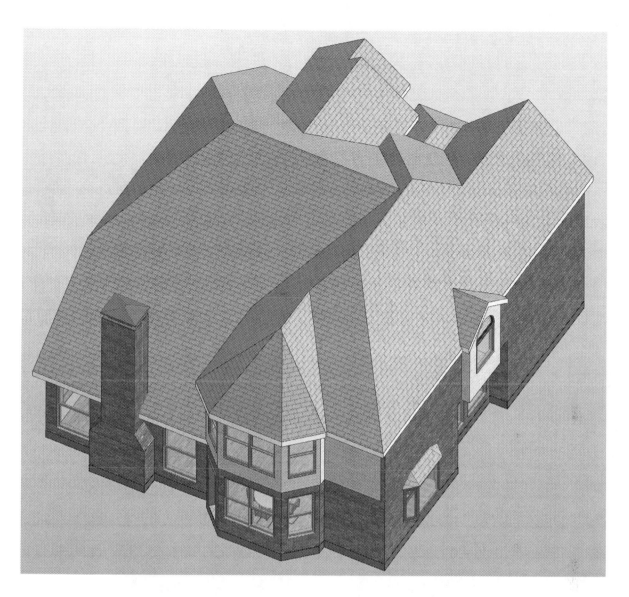

Figure 33.5. Rear bird's-eye view of completed house roof

Conclusion

You now have a formidable arsenal of tools and techniques to use in realistically modeling even a fairly complex residential roof. With a little practice, you will be able to tackle any roof-modeling project without being at all intimidated by its complexity. Knowledge is power, and you have greatly enlarged your store of knowledge by going through the exercises in this book.

We've come a long way since we started examining Revit's basic roof-modeling tools and discussed how to model a simple shed roof over a pump house. I hope that this in-depth exploration of Revit's considerable array of roof-building tools has clearly demonstrated that Revit has powerful capabilities that can be put to excellent use on residential projects. And with time, Revit will get even better.

With study and practice, using the tools and techniques covered in this book, you can become the person who clients and teammates go to for knowledge of how to model and detail even a complex house roof.

Revit is a very deep and robust software tool, with many levels to explore and learn about. I learn new tricks every day; that's part of the fun.

I encourage you to join and be active in Revit discussion groups and subscribe to Revit blogs (including BestCADtips.com!) to regularly keep adding to your knowledge.

If you found this book helpful, please tell your friends and coworkers about it, take a minute to give us an online review, and share your thoughts about the book in your social media meeting places.

Here's to your continued success modeling residential projects with Revit!

Image Credits

All Autodesk Revit screenshots are reprinted courtesy of Autodesk, Inc. Additional permissions are as follows:

Figure 0.2	Used by permission of Plans By Design—Randy Cox (http://www.plansbydesign.com/)
Figure 1.1	Used by permission of A.T.S. Design—Joseph Kirby (http://cooltheaters.net/)
Figure 2.5-A	Used by permission of Plans By Design—Randy Cox (http://www.plansbydesign.com/)
Figure 2.6	Used by permission of Plans By Design—Randy Cox (http://www.plansbydesign.com/)

All photographic images, illustrations, tables, and diagrams are by the author, with the following exceptions:

Figure 12.1	Public Domain via Pixabay / https://pixabay.com
Figure 15.1	Photo by tpsdave, Public Domain via Pixabay / https://pixabay.com
Figure 17.1	Public Domain via Pixabay / https://pixabay.com and Wikimedia Commons / https://commons.wikimedia.org
Figure 19.1	Photo by Darryl Brooks (/gallery-60503p1.html), licensed through Shutterstock (http://www.shutterstock.com/)

Suggestions for Further Reading

Burden, Ernest. *Illustrated Dictionary of Architecture*. New York: McGraw-Hill, 2002.

Ching, Francis D. K. *Building Construction Illustrated*. New York: Van Nostrand Reinhold, 1975.

Kicklighter, Clois E., et al. *Architecture: Residential Drawing and Design.* South Holland, IL: Goodheart-Willcox, 1995.

McAlester, Virginia and Lee. *A Field Guide to American Houses.* New York: Alfred A. Knopf, 1991.

Printed in the United States
By Bookmasters